GOD
REFLECTED
METAPHORS FOR LIFE

FLORA A. KESHGEGIAN

To Louisa,
Many blessings for
your journey of faith.
Flora A. Keshgegian

FORTRESS PRESS
MINNEAPOLIS

GOD REFLECTED
Metaphors for Life

Cover image: *Cadmium Orange Bridge*, Oneida Creek, by Richard Kathmann © 2001 Richard Kathmann. Photo by James Demarest. Used by permission.

Cover design: Christa Rubsam
Book design: Douglas Schmitz

Library of Congress Cataloging-in-Publication Data
Keshgegian, Flora A., 1950-
  God reflected: metaphors for life / Flora A. Keshgegian.
    p. cm.
  Includes index.
  ISBN 978-0-8006-6254-7 (alk. paper)
  1. God (Christianity) I. Title.
  BT103.K463 2008
  231.7—dc22
                    2007036827

The paper used in this publication meets the minimum requirements of American National Standard for Information Sciences—Permanence of Paper for Printed Library Materials, ANSI Z329.48-1984.

Manufactured in the U.S.A.

12   11   10   09   08   1   2   3   4   5   6   7   8   9   10

For my students
who asked questions

and for all those who seek to understand

CONTENTS

PREFACE

A S A THEOLOGIAN AND ORDAINED MINISTER, I have a recurring experience. I am at a party or social gathering. Someone, often a person I just met, approaches me and wants to talk about God. That person tells me that he used to believe in God, but then his thirty-four-year-old brother, with a wife and two young children, was diagnosed with terminal cancer. How could God be that cruel, he asks me? What kind of God does that? Or a woman tells me that, after much internal confusion and a long struggle, she came to the realization that she is lesbian. Now the Christians she knows tell her she is not acceptable to God. I feel God does accept me, she says. In fact, I think God helped me to know myself. Am I right about God, or are those who tell me God condemns who I am right? Or the person at the party tells me that everyone in his family remains very active in the church in which he grew up, but now, when he attends, the worship seems hollow, the words meaningless. The God I hear about in church, he says, seems so distant and different from my life. Is there something wrong with me? Still others ask about what is happening in the world today and what God is doing about such things. Where was God on 9/11, they may ask. Or they may say, I don't understand why we have to worry about global warming. Isn't God going to bring everything to an end anyway? What do you think?

When I teach or lead workshops, students and participants also ask questions. Sometimes they feel confused about hearing something different from what they always thought was true. Or they are beginning to question and reflect on their own theological positions. Or they want to understand the meaning of faith statements they have recited for years.

I am thrilled when people ask questions and search for answers. That means they are beginning the task of theology. One of the oldest definitions of theology is "faith seeking understanding." Asking questions, reflecting on faith, and thinking critically are all part of faith seeking understanding, of the search for truth and for faith that is meaningful and life-giving.

I wrote this book for those seeking such faith. I hope it provides food for their journeys of exploration. All the people who have questioned me about God and all those students who wanted to understand contributed to what is in these pages, and I thank them. They helped me to find ways to articulate and make sense of the logic of faith statements and theological affirmations.

I am grateful to a number of individuals as well: Kay Johnson, Barbara Radtke and Sherilyn Pearce, who read the manuscript and offered their thoughtful perspectives and suggestions, for their generosity and support; David Jensen for commenting so astutely on a key chapter; Carol Brorsen for reading parts of the manuscript and prompting me to think about audience; and from Fortress Press, J. Michael West for his enthusiastic support and his editorial wisdom and Susan Johnson and Carolyn Banks for their diligence and gracious guidance. I am ever thankful as well for my family and friends who sustain me and bring joy to my life.

INTRODUCTION

SEEKING GOD'S WILL

*"Our Father in heaven
hallowed be your Name,
your kingdom come,
your will be done,
on earth as in heaven."*

W HETHER CHRISTIANS PRAY ALONE or gather together for worship, they often recite "The Lord's Prayer." These words serve as a statement of faith for them, naming who God is, how God acts, and who they are in relation to God. The prayer begins by addressing God as father, "our Father." Then the prayer asks that God's kingdom and rule be established throughout the universe. In the opening lines, God is imagined to be like a male parent and also like a king.

Then the prayer states that God's "will be done, on earth as in heaven." Those who pray these words desire God's will, which rules in heaven, to direct human existence on earth as well. God's will—seeking to know it and desiring to live according to it—is at the heart of Christian faith and prayer for so many people. They not only imagine God as a father and king ruling all things, but also believe God *is* father and ruler of the universe. God's will directs; it will prevail. Christians pray for that dominion.

Sounds simple and straightforward. Yet wars have been fought and churches divided over what God is believed to want and to will. My goal in this book is to get inside these assertions, images, and beliefs in order to explore what is being said about who God is and how God acts, especially in light of conflicting claims made about God and God's will in the world in which we live.

I invite readers to reflect on such questions as: Who is the God to whom Christians pray and whose will Christians seek? What is God like? How does God act? What is meant by God's will? What kinds of claims are made for it? How is God's will an expression of who God is? This introduction opens up such questions by looking at different meanings of God's will.

When Bad Things Happen

One afternoon in February 2005, twin sisters, Kayla and Rachel, fourteen years old, went out on horseback at a riding club in southeastern Massachusetts. Kayla's horse reared back, threw her off and then fell on top of her. She was pronounced dead soon after being taken to the hospital. Rachel was unharmed. Two sisters, equally accomplished, engaged in the same activity but experienced a very different outcome. *The Providence Journal* article reporting this tragedy quoted the twins' mother: "It was just a freak accident. . . . There's no rhyme or reason to it. It just happened." Toward the end of the same article, the young girl's godmother, her aunt, is quoted: "God must have needed another angel . . . that's why he took our Kayla."

Mother and godmother offered very different interpretations of the same event. One emphasized the tragic nature of the accident and its random nature; the other gave the death a reason and a purpose. She claimed it to be God's action. The mother suggested there was no answer to the question "why"; the godmother believed that God's will was the answer.

In December 2004 an earthquake in the middle of the Indian Ocean generated a giant tsunami that hit islands and the coastlines of numerous South Asian countries. More than 175,000 people died as a result. Many, many more were injured, left homeless and bereft. People the world over asked why this terrible thing had happened. How could God let such a tragedy befall so many innocent people? Others wondered what God was saying to the world through this mighty act of destruction.

Similar questions were raised in 2005 when Hurricane Katrina swept over the Louisiana and Mississippi coastlines and submerged much of the city of New Orleans. As some observers suggested, was this event, life shattering for tens of thousands of people and immensely destructive, evidence of God's judgment?

Americans experienced September 11, 2001, as a day of terror and horror. Many people died in the attacks on the World Trade Center and the collapse of its twin towers. More people were killed in rescue efforts, as well as in the attack on the Pentagon and in the downed airplane in Pennsylvania. Survivors, in recounting their ordeal, reported praying to God for deliverance and thanking God for being spared. They spoke of "miracles" that put just the right person in the right place at the right moment to help them down the stairs or to lead them to an open passageway. No doubt many of those who died prayed to God as well. Why would God intervene to spare one person and not the other? What does it mean for a survivor to claim that God worked a miracle on his behalf, when God did not act to save the person in the next office or on the next floor?

A friend dies of cancer after several years of fighting for her life. In all the ups and downs of the disease, she prayed to God. Each hint of remission was perceived as a gift from God, a possible miracle. Each setback brought questions about God's intent and why this was happening. Upon her death, mourners attest to her faith and courage. They also try to find comfort through such expressions as: It was God's will. It was her time. She is in a better place now.

From the point of view of the central characters, each of these events and stories is about suffering and death, undeserved and untimely. Perhaps for as long as human beings have walked this earth and had thoughts about their lives, they have asked the question why. This question seems especially to arise, to borrow Harold S. Kushner's book title, when bad things happen to good people.

All the world's religions, including Christianity, address the question of suffering in some way. Each religion—whether a major religious tradition such as Buddhism or an indigenous or popular religious practice such as Voodoo—offers answers and ways to deal with suffering and loss, tragedy and death. Those responses include attention to the feelings of vulnerability and powerlessness evoked by suffering and loss.

Christianity, along with Judaism and Islam, assert there is one God who is supreme and mighty. These religions turn to that one God for answers. They draw upon ideas about the sovereignty of God in order to respond to unjust suffering, untimely death, and tragedy. God's will is often at the center of any such responses. It is key to understanding why bad things happen and why people suffer. God is the shield against the potential chaos and meaninglessness of existence.

The sovereign God is both present and active. Among God's attributes are power and goodness. God is all powerful, as well as all good and all loving. Therefore, we can trust that everything is in God's good and mighty hands.

In Rabbi Kushner's title, *When Bad Things Happen to Good People*, there is no one directing the action, no agent. Bad things occur; no one seems to be making them happen. However, many people who ask questions in such moments, especially those who do so from within a religion such as Christianity, tend to put their questions in the active voice and add in an agent: "Why does God make or allow bad things to happen to good people? Why did God give me cancer? Why did God cause a tsunami that killed so many people?" God is the one willing and intending, acting and guiding.

God's Will for the World

In many strains of Christian thinking, God's will is manifest not only in times of suffering or disaster but in everything that happens in the world and even in the universe. All that exists and everything that occurs is an expression of God's will.

This idea is rooted in the basic affirmations of monotheism: that God is the creator, sustainer, and redeemer of the world. Beginning with creation, then continuing with God's providential care, as well as God's work of redemption and of bringing all things to completion, God's guiding will is at work. All that exists, including time and history, originate from God. God directs history and creation toward their God-intended ends. God is the beginning and the end. God's will is always good, always right.

Those who live within such a narrative and belief system are able, therefore, to understand their lives and what happens in them as meaningful and purposeful. Life events are not random occurrences in a chaotic universe. They are God's own doing.

The song, "He's Got the Whole World in His Hands," offers such an image: God holds and cares for each and every person and all of creation. But God's hands are not only images of care and support. They also signify action and direction. God's "hands" shape and mold, intervene and cause change. The book of Exodus states that God's mighty hand parted the waters of the Red Sea so that the Israelites might escape from slavery in Egypt. The prophetic literature claims that God is able to make a way for Israel to return from its exile in Babylon. For many Christians the chief evidence of God's power and care is the resurrection: God raises Jesus from the dead, and God will also raise all who have been saved.

Within the biblical story, testimony is offered again and again not only to such mighty acts of God but also to the specificity and expanse of God's knowledge and providence. God is present just as much in the details. God knows the number of hairs on people's heads; no sparrow falls without God's awareness and involvement. Even on this minute level of detail, God's presence and intent is manifest.

God's will, God's purposeful activity, is thus an overriding and underlying message of the Jewish and Christian faith traditions that claim the biblical story as their own. In those traditions, faith in God means confidence in God's power, including the power of God's actions and God's will. God will prevail. God's purposes will be realized. God's will not only acts in and through human lives but it is effective throughout time and space. The affirmation that God is an able agent who is powerful and good seems to be a bedrock of biblical faith.

To be faithful means to seek and follow God's will. For thousands of years people of faith have searched for God's will in their lives and asked God to order their lives according to that will. Faithfulness was marked by conformity to God's will.

For all those years, religious and political leaders have been concerned with God's will in and for the world. They make public claims for God's will and declare that they are following God's will. For example, some of the founders and architects of America thought God was at work in what they were doing. The "doctrine of manifest destiny" holds that America has an intended purpose, determined by God. America is destined to be a beacon of freedom and democracy for the world. It is a world power, directing and leading other nations who are not so richly blessed. The doctrine of manifest destiny also implies that power and success are signs of God's favor. America is God's chosen nation and American politicians profess their actions as aligned with God's purposes for this country.

Such American claims do not go unchallenged. Other peoples and nations also believe that God is directing them to accomplish God's will. Even though it is difficult for many to imagine, those who planned and executed the attacks of September 11 believed they were following God's will and fulfilling God's purposes. To consider oneself the chosen of God, whether as a person or as a nation, produces a sense of mission and of having a special status. One's actions are justified and even blessed because their source is God's own intent. How then should such claims, especially when they are in conflict, be evaluated and assessed?

"God Willing"

Thus far I have described God's will in relation to moments of suffering and crisis and in relation to major events in people's lives, in history, and even in the universe. For those who seek to be faithful to God, concern about God's will is also an everyday matter. Many of the forms of daily prayer, such as "The Lord's Prayer," reflect this attitude of living in the presence of God, directed by God's will. When people thank God upon arising in the morning or when they say grace at a meal or when they ask God to keep them safe through the night, they are recognizing all they do and all that happens as under God's guidance and care. Attaching the phrase "God willing" to plans to meet for lunch next Wednesday or to getting all one's daily tasks accomplished is an expression of this living in and by God's will in the everyday.

In the modern and postmodern world, many people go about their daily lives with a more secular sensibility, which is to say they are not consciously attentive to God's presence and action in every moment, every undertaking. This lack of constant awareness of God is a key aspect of secularity. In medieval times the church was the center of communal life. As peasants worked in the fields, the church bells would sound several times a day. The bells were a call to prayer. Workers would stop what they were doing in order to turn their attention to God and to God's presence and purpose in their lives. They would acknowledge God as the one to whom all things belonged. Everything was God's domain. All was under God's dominion.

Today, people's lives are different. Even if they pray each day, those days are no longer marked by the call of church bells. People may even turn their thoughts to God several times a day, but unless they live in a religious community, their days are not structured around those times. However, whether people pray daily or not, or in whatever form, if they maintain that God is the one directing their lives, they understand God's will to be guiding and determining. And when something happens to disturb their everyday lives, they wonder why. They wonder what God might be up to.

People seek for God's will for their lives not only in moments of uncertainty and turmoil but also in times of transition and decision. They may ask God whom they are meant to marry. They may look for God's guidance about a job offer or a career choice. They may search the scripture for clues or meditate quietly or look for some sign in unfolding events.

People also ask God to give them what they want and need. In praying for a safe and successful operation, they want God to direct the skill of the surgical team. In praying for guidance in a decision, they want God to make the outcome a good one for them. People's requests often are straightforward. They petition God: Heal my child. Find me a job. Make my marriage better. Help me hit a home run. Whether a prayer focuses on a matter of life or death or on what might be considered a trivial request, the desire expressed is that God's will be the same as the will of the one praying. People want God to fulfill their wants.

People not only pray for themselves but ask others to pray for them. And they pray for others in turn. Prayers may be offered for loved ones but also for strangers or for those continents away. In such cases people are not praying that God's will be manifest in their own lives but in others' lives. The gesture of praying for others suggests that God's will extends broadly. God's care embraces the whole world and all that is in it. God holds everyone in God's hands.

Whatever people pray for—whether it be for good health or home runs, for themselves or for others—they do so assuming that God hears and answers prayer. What does such an assumption suggest about who God is and how God's will operates? Because prayer is at the heart of how people relate to God, this book explores the different ways in which people approach God in prayer and what expectations and assumptions about God they bring to that activity.

The Flow of the Book

There is no one way to imagine God, no one way to understand God's will. To be sure, to propose that God has a will would seem to mean that God is like a person, most often imaged as father or lord. Expressions, such as "the guiding hand of God" or "the commanding voice of God" or even "the mind of God," all suggest that the divine operates like a human person. They imply that God has hands and a voice and a brain and that God exercises agency. These ways of talking about God reflect an anthropomorphic view of God, that is, God imaged in human terms. What kind of person is God? Does God have to be imaged as a person? Or as father? What happens if we understand these ways of imagining God as metaphors?

A basic assumption of this book, which will be explored in the next chapter, is that what we know and imagine about God is metaphorical, which is to say it is more approximation than actual description. Even the concept of God's will is a metaphor. Another assumption is that Christians, in the past or present, have employed a variety of ways to imagine God, but some of these have received short shrift. This book seeks to explore a wide range of metaphors and images. It asks of these ways of imagining God: What is God like? How does God relate to us and to everything that God created? In particular, what kind of power does God exercise and how does God exercise it?

Chapters 2 through 8 of this book are each devoted to one approach, one understanding of who God is, how God acts, and how God's will is perceived. The chapters flow in a particular direction, from views of God's will that emphasize God's power as commanding and determinative, through views that soften God's use of power and seek to imagine it more in harmony with human power, to views of God that are less anthropomorphic and less directing. My own preference, as will be evident in the argument of the book, is for a view of God as energy for life. This God desires what is life-giving and promoting but does not will things per se.

- Chapter 1 orients the reader to what it means to talk about God and God's will as metaphor. It considers the tasks of theology and the nature of language about God.

- Chapter 2 is devoted to examining a monarchial view of God as king and lord. God's will is all powerful and all determining.

- Chapter 3 examines a patriarchal view of God as a commanding and ruling father. God's will orders and directs all of life.

- Chapter 4 focuses on the patriarchal God, as fully powerful, but more prone to mercy. God's will is expressed in compassion, as well as justice.

- Chapter 5 turns to attempts to soften the force of God's will as determinative. God the father is more like a nurturing parent, whose will is to coach us through persuasion and to support our freedom.

- Chapter 6 attends to views of God not as intending suffering but as present in and with suffering. God suffers with us and cares for us in suffering. God's will is expressed as compassion, companionship, and resistance.

- Chapter 7 explores the nature of God as relational. This God shares power and expresses power through us. God's will seeks cooperation.

- Chapter 8 moves away from a personal God to a view of the divine as the energy of connection and life in the universe. This God is no longer characterized by notions of personal agency or a guiding will.

- Chapter 9 reviews the movement of the book and discusses the implications for how we might live if we reimagine God and God's will.

I invite readers to join in this exploration. May readers find resources in this book for their own journey with God. May they feel moved to give voice to their experiences and to examine their views. And may they grow in knowledge and wisdom.

1

GOD THE METAPHOR
IMAGING GOD

Y EARS AGO I EXPERIENCED ONE of those moments that remains with you for a lifetime. It was not something I would have predicted. I was among a group of people talking about God. A woman was speaking. She insisted that God was "Father," a patriarch at the top of a hierarchical universe, created and directed by God. This God was powerful and in charge of everything. Such was the nature of reality. Otherwise, the speaker suggested, the universe would not be right.

I knew this speaker. She was a professor at a local college and an active Episcopalian. In fact, she was a strong advocate of the efforts of women to be ordained. At that time, as one of the women in the Episcopal church seeking ordination to the priesthood, I had come to count on this woman as someone who would argue strongly for the inclusion and equality of women in all forms of church leadership.

So I felt confused by her emphatic assertion, offered with such passion. Why would someone who was so supportive of women's leadership continue to see God as a male and a patriarch? Why did someone who was advocating change in the church have such an unchanging image of God? Her beliefs surprised me, especially since I wanted the church to reconsider such exclusive male imagery and language for God. What surprised me more was what happened next.

In that moment I had a different vision of God. In my mind's eye I saw energy, manifest as flashes of light, in constant motion. Nothing was static in this universe. The flashes of light, like stars in motion against a night sky, were going in many directions at once. They were connecting and creating connections across space and time. What seemed most real in this universe was energy, ever in motion. God, the divine, was the energy itself, dynamic and connecting.

This vision offered a very different view of God than the one the professor had just described. She saw God as a male person; my image was not of a person at all. Her God ruled over a set and static order. In my vision the divine was not only in constant motion but was the motion itself. In the professor's universe God gave everything an assigned place in a hierarchy. My imagined universe was not hierarchical but relational, multidimensional, and even random.

I did not tell anyone about this vision when it happened. Nor did I speak about it for a long time. Even though I felt that what I had seen in my mind's eye was true—indeed more true than the father God atop a hierarchical universe—I was afraid to say anything. My image of God seemed so different from what I had been taught and what others declared was true. How would it be received?

I did not know why I imagined God in that way. Nor could I point to a source for my vision. I did not even know how to talk about what I had experienced. I felt as if I had had an insight into the being of God, into the nature of the divine, but I had little language to describe it. I had no context for understanding it. And I had few resources for expressing it. As a result, even though I knew what I had seen in my mind's eye, I could not fully claim this vision.

I struggled, before and after that experience, with the image of God as father, the patriarchal head of a universe that "he" creates and governs. My problems with this image were several. I had difficulty enough with an image of God as male. It seemed too narrow and exclusionary to me. But I also had questions about the nature of God's personhood. God was said to be a person, but "he" was not like us. God chose to create us, but God did not have to. Nor did God need us or anything outside of "himself."

I could not make good sense of this view of God as totally other and noncontingent, to use the theological term. To be contingent means to be related to, to be affected by, to touch and be touched. This patriarchal God was beyond affect and interrelation. This God did not allow touching.

I also resisted the idea of a set world order, established by God and therefore sacred. The idea that God had willed a hierarchical universe seemed too politically convenient for those in power, that is, for those at the top of the hierarchy. They claimed God's power to back up their own. At the same time such hierarchical ordering was too onerous for those at the bottom. It afforded them little access to power and few resources for changing the way things were.

In fact, this ordered universe also turned out to be static: The essence of God's nature was to be unchanging. If God was unchanging then God would be opposed to change in the world as well, especially when change seemed to threaten the God given order. God's will, the patriarchal will, had created everything and ordered it in set ways. To advocate change meant to oppose God's will. This aversion to change also turned out to be politically convenient for those in power. They could argue: If God had intended the social order to be different, would not God have created it that way?

Motivated by such concerns and struggles, I continued to study theology. In the course of my studies I discovered feminist theology and was drawn to it as a helpful, clarifying, and affirming resource. Feminist theology, as it developed in the 1970s and into the 80s and 90s, raised many questions about traditional images of God and the ways in which God was depicted and defined. It also undertook to reimagine the divine.

Feminist theologians pointed out that the images used for God tended to serve the interests of males who were dominant in the social order. Those images reinforced patriarchal social patterns. If God was a patriarch in a hierarchically ordered universe, which was created and sanctioned by God, then, feminist theologians pointed out, it was difficult to argue for more egalitarian perspectives, especially for women and others not at the top of the hierarchy.

It was also difficult to challenge long held ideas of what women should and should not do. For example, if priests were literally to image

Jesus Christ, as Roman Catholics and others argued, then women could not be priests. If families were to reflect the God-given order, then wives were to be subject to their husbands. To challenge these traditional norms was to disobey God, to oppose God's will.

Feminist theologians, however, along with others who were questioning the political biases of traditional views, also began to imagine God differently. What if God were not at the top of a hierarchical universe? Perhaps God was female. Or not gendered. What if God were not imaged as a person at all? Suppose change was a good thing, a necessary thing, for those who felt as if the given social order was harmful to their well-being. Might change then be perceived as God-given or even as part of the nature of God?

These theologians not only asked questions but they began to offer alternative images that were more dynamic. They expanded the gender of God to include female images and opened up thinking about gender itself and about personhood. Was it the nature of women to be more caring and men more detached? Or were such characteristics a result of the ways males and females had been raised to be? Might God then be imagined as a commanding woman or a nurturing man? These theologians went even further to suggest that God did not always have to be depicted with human characteristics. They paid more attention to God as evidenced throughout the created order: for example, they found images in the bible of God as wind or light.

Some feminist theologians spoke about God as relational and as wanting and making real connection. What was most true of God had to do with relationship and connection, energy and change. God was affected by what was outside of or other than God. God did want to touch and to be touched. In these ways, feminist theology began to provide language I could draw upon to talk about the vision I had experienced. It also helped me to feel less solitary in my perspective.

However, it was not until I began to learn about quantum physics and its view of the universe that I found a worldview fully supportive of my vision. In the world of quantum physics, the ultimate reality in the universe is dynamic energy. When Albert Einstein argued that $E = mc^2$, he began a revolution in our thinking. Since then, physicists have been moving more and more away from a Newtonian universe of fixed laws and concrete matter to a universe alive with energy in motion. What we know as solid and material, such as the chair I am sitting on as I write these words, is actually dynamic energy materialized into the particular substance of wood that is then formed and shaped to constitute a chair. If, as Einstein argued, the chair began moving at the speed of light, it would transform into energy.

Quantum physics is a highly abstract discipline. Its worldview is difficult to grasp. I take from it, though, a few rather simple and straightforward principles. Along with seeing the essence of reality as energy, I understand that the universe is ever dynamic and not static. Not only change but also a kind of indeterminacy characterizes the universe. The patriarchal God whose will rules and determines everything does not make sense in such a universe. Nor does a view of the order of the universe as fixed and unchanging.

Although there is a kind of order in the world of quantum physics, such ordering is also dynamic. We might imagine it as webs of connection and interdependence. Motion in any one place affects the whole. My vision of flashes of light, ever moving, indeterminate and dynamic, offers an image that might better approximate the nature of God in such a universe. Nothing, not even God, is static or fixed.

That vision came to me some thirty years ago, but I have been living into it ever since I experienced it. It has taken root in both my theological and spiritual journey. Along the way I have found resources and companions that have helped me understand it more fully, giving it more shape and definition. This book is fruit of that journey.

How We Know and Imagine God

What any one of us knows of God originated in someone's experience, someone's imagination. We cannot think about God without using our imaginations. Anything we say about God, or that others have said, including what is recorded in scripture, is formed and informed by what is imaginable.

The word *theology* literally means "God-talk." In general terms theology consists of describing who God, or the divine, is; what God/ divine does; and what difference that makes for human beings and for the world. Theology is a human endeavor, an intellectual, conceptual activity that relies on language. In other words, in order to "do" theology, theologians need to be able to think, to imagine, and to give expression to their thoughts and imaginings in language. These are the tools theologians have available. These tools allow theologians, and all of us, to talk about God and to know God. But they also set limits on who God is and what we know about God. Our understanding of God is limited by what we can think, imagine, and say.

At the heart of the work of theology is this dilemma: God, the divine, is that which by its nature is beyond the limitations of human understanding, imagination, and language. And yet, theologians have asserted, God wants to be known and so God reveals Godself in and to the world. God is also that which human beings seek to know, intimately and truly.

In traditional terms God is both transcendent and immanent. As transcendent, God is beyond or outside of human experience and knowledge. God is totally other, not like us humans. As immanent, God is in our midst, among us and even in us. God is like us, intimately present. Historically and still today theologians have tended to perceive God's transcendence and immanence as opposed or in tension. Most theologians have favored transcendence; fewer have favored immanence. Some have sought to view these two dimensions of God in relation, but usually, and in the end, these theologians put more value on transcendence.

As a result, Christianity, the religion that claims God became incarnate in the person of Jesus, that God was present in human flesh, has remained wary of the immanence implied by incarnation. This is one of the ironies of Christian theology. In its central theological tenet, Christianity affirms immanence at the same time that it eschews it. The early church theologians who insisted that Jesus was divine "in the flesh" also believed in a God who was fully transcendent and other, not like humans. They had difficulty holding these two beliefs together.

Another traditional theological affirmation is that God, the divine, is mystery. I prefer this way of thinking about God to the language of transcendence and immanence. To speak of God as mystery avoids the opposition that the terms transcendence and immanence tend to set up. To say that God is mystery is to acknowledge that God is in some sense unknowable or that we cannot fully know God.

Yet, at the same time, the term communicates our desire for God, to know and be known. Mystery draws us in. What is unknown is alluring, even if somewhat unsettling. God as mystery attracts. Such a view of God also reminds us of our limitations, our inability to fully comprehend.

Approaching God as mystery is like the experience of being in love. When we fall in love with someone we want to be totally intimate with that person, to know them from the inside out, to be connected as deeply and fully as we can be. We also realize, however, that no matter how much the other person shares of himself or herself with us and we with him or her, no matter how much time we spend together and how many experiences we share, there will remain a part of each of us that is mysterious, and other, to one another. This enduring mystery, however, attracts us even more and we yearn for full union, a way to be one.

These dynamics that characterize the knowledge of lovers are even more the case in knowing God. The more we know, the more intimately present we are with God and God with us, the more we realize that there is a vast mystery we have not even touched. And then we find ourselves wanting to know even more of God, to draw ever closer.

In this way, our experiencing, learning about, and reflecting upon God is a never ending, never completed, never exhausted endeavor. We turn to the sources we have available for such knowledge: our own experiences; the written testimony of others as present in scripture; the history of the Christian community and what the wisdom of that tradition practices and says about God; and the wisdom present in other traditions and arenas of knowledge, such as the sciences or poetry or art, as well as other religions. We draw upon whatever is available to us to satisfy the thirst we experience for the living God. In turn, we add to those resources by giving expression to what we come to know of God.

Metaphor and Language

Because God is, first and last, mystery, whatever language we use to speak about God, whatever images we might conjure up, whatever assertions we state to be true, even absolutely true, are forms of metaphor. They are an approximation, a comparison, an analogy. Metaphorical language posits a relationship between one thing and another. For example, the statement "she's a wet blanket" suggests a relationship between a woman and a wet blanket. The phrase refers to the woman's behavior or attitude, which has the quality of a wet blanket used to put out a fire. The metaphor suggests that this woman's behavior dampens enthusiasm or stifles energy, but it is not meant literally. The woman is neither wet nor a blanket. "Wet blanket" is used suggestively. It is an evocative image. Another example of metaphor is: "She is a breath of fresh air." Again, this is not meant literally. The woman is not made of air. We do not experience her as breath. Rather, we are saying that her presence is refreshing and enlivening. It may also provide clarity, a new perspective or new energy. The economy of metaphor is such that a metaphor is able to convey, in a word or two, significantly more meaning.

Metaphors may even evoke whole worlds. For example, we may describe someone as a wizard in the kitchen. The term *wizard* conjures up the realm of magic and sorcery. The metaphor suggests that the cook's abilities are particularly impressive, that he is able to put together ingredients to produce a tasty dish and do so in a way that seems easy and perhaps surprising. The cook is not actually using magic, but what he is able to do seems to go beyond the ordinary, so much so that we call upon the extraordinary to describe it.

A biblical metaphor for God, found especially in the psalms, is rock: "my God, my rock in whom I take refuge" (Psalm 18:2). The psalmist who voiced that affirmation is not suggesting that rocks are divine or that we should worship rocks. However, imagining God as a rock allows the psalmist to give voice to a particular understanding or experience of God. Perhaps it is a sense of solidity or stability or endurance. Or perhaps it is the kind of shelter that rock caves offered in the desert landscape of ancient Israel. God as a rock provides a refuge, a place to be safe from one's enemies or the elements.

A key term in metaphorical statements is "like," though the word itself is not often stated directly, except in similes. A metaphor is able to compare one thing to another because there is a similarity, a connection, a likeness, between the two things. A metaphor does not work if the connection or likeness seems too implausible. It does not make sense, for example, to describe a powerful person as having the force of a feather. For most of us, feathers represent weakness. They are light and blow away easily.

Once we recognize the metaphorical nature of the language we use to imagine and talk about God, it is helpful to explore further what that recognition implies. First of all, it suggests that metaphors come from our imaginations. Metaphors presume the ability to imagine and to draw comparisons. To say that God is a rock is to be able to imagine God in that way, as solid and enduring, as a refuge.

The more rich, free, varied, and practiced our imaginations are, the more expansively we will be able to imagine God. In Islam there is a tradition of the ninety-nine names of God. Among them are the Guardian, the Bestower, the Utterly Just, the Reckoner, the Light. The ninety-nine names illuminate and point to a variety of metaphors and attributes for Allah. Such a list suggests that Allah is so great that our names for God cannot be exhausted. Muslims recite or chant the ninety-nine names as a devotional practice to help them recognize the majesty and greatness of Allah. It may be a helpful exercise for our own imaginations to try to come up with ninety-nine names or metaphors for God.

Another point to keep in mind is that metaphors are only effective if the comparison and connection they make works. I have already suggested that metaphors function best when the connection—the likeness—is easy to apprehend and makes sense. It needs to be believable. The most believable metaphors draw on things in our experience. Otherwise, we cannot relate to them. For example, if we had lived on the western plains of the United States in the nineteenth century, describing the power of God as thundering buffalo would have been a suggestive and useful metaphor. Today that experience is no longer available and the metaphor seems startling and even shocking.

Metaphorical language implies dissimilarity, as well as similarity, in the comparison. If there were no dissimilarity, then the metaphor would be in danger of collapsing and becoming one with what it describes. This happens with metaphors for God, especially ones such as father. Numerous theologians have argued that God *is* father, not metaphorically but actually. Other metaphors for God, such as rock, are not as vulnerable to this danger.

Another important factor in thinking about metaphors is culture. Metaphors for God need to make sense culturally. The more restrictive the culture, the more limited will be the range of metaphors used. For example, if, in our cultural experience, women are never in leadership and are marked as weak and dependent, then it will be difficult to imagine God as female or to offer an image of God as mighty as a woman's arm. Because the cultures of the western world in which Christianity developed have been so androcentric—that is, male-centered—there are few examples of female metaphors for God. Those that do exist are limited to attributes and activities culturally identified as feminine, such as giving birth or tending to children. For example, when medieval mystic Julian of Norwich named Jesus as our mother, she was emphasizing the nurturing care of Jesus.

But however restrictive a culture may be and however strong a dominant culture may seem, there are always a variety of subcultures present in any society. Culture is a complex and multifaceted phenomenon that cannot be defined solely by its dominant aspects. The way in which a particular metaphor or image is viewed and valued may well depend on a person's social position and cultural location. Take, for example, the trickster figure found in many folk tales, such as the adventures of Brer Rabbit. To those in power, the trickster is a problematic figure, seen not as virtuous or good, but as causing chaos and acting inappropriately. Those who do not have access to social power, however, see tricksters as adept at finding a way to what is life-giving despite obstacles and difficulties. Tricksters are clever and proficient at getting around the powers that be. For those with little social and political power, imaging God as a trickster may be an effective metaphor, a positive image; for those more powerful, it might be a quite disagreeable one.

The metaphors we use often reflect only certain perspectives. They may represent biased points of view and limited political interests. For example, as we have become more aware of racial prejudice in our culture, we have also become more sensitive to the ways in which we use metaphors of light and dark. Valued, positive, good things are described as light while negative, bad things are described as dark. When someone is in a bad mood, we often say there is a dark cloud hanging over him (rather than saying a "rain cloud"). When someone makes us happy, we say she lights up our day (rather than saying she is like a "sunny day"). An exercise to help us get a sense of just how conditioned we are to this way of thinking would be to spend five minutes listing positive metaphors of lightness and then five minutes listing positive metaphors of darkness. My hunch is that the lists would be very different in length.

Metaphors are always culturally specific. Sometimes when the cultural context shifts, metaphors may not work as well. Other times they are used to bolster certain social realities. For example, imaging God as male has functioned again and again to reinforce men's claims to power and dominance and to exclude and subordinate women. Much of the language used for God in the Bible is also monarchial: God is lord, king, and sovereign. Such metaphors have a different resonance in America, which rebelled against a monarchy and has a democratic, elected form of government. So what does it mean when Americans name God as king and sovereign? How are they imagining their relationship with God?

All metaphors are ultimately limited and inadequate. They can only approximate the reality we may be trying to describe and the truth we are trying to convey. If we have ever tried to express fully and adequately something deeply felt, such as the love we have for a partner or a child, we may well understand how inadequate even the best metaphors are. At the same time that we need metaphors to enable us to communicate the depth and breadth of what we know, we also realize that we can never do so as well as we would like. When it comes to talking about God, all language about God is a form of metaphor. These metaphors both help us know God and they fall short of such knowledge.

Still, metaphors are powerful. As I have suggested they not only express and reflect what we are trying to convey, but they shape our thinking, imagining, and even acting. Some of the most powerful metaphors are not even recognized as such. Often the most powerful metaphors are so embedded in our worldview and are so central to it, that they function like the air we breathe. We breathe all the time, but most of the time, we are not conscious of breathing. We are always taking in air, breathing in and out, but we neither recognize that we are surrounded by air nor that we constantly interact with it.

Some spiritual practitioners, especially teachers of yoga and meditation techniques, are helping us become more conscious of our breathing. Just as they believe that such attention will enable us to live our lives better and more faithfully, I think that it is helpful to recognize the metaphors that shape our lives, including how they are used and the role they play in guiding our beliefs and actions. The more ubiquitous a metaphor is and the more we take it for granted, the more we need to pay conscious attention. Perhaps we even need to practice paying attention in order to perceive its metaphoric nature.

We also become aware of our breath when we have trouble breathing. Similarly, we may become aware of the metaphoric nature of a concept that we take for granted, when it no longer works as expected or promised. I implied in the introduction that we begin to question God's will when something especially difficult or bad happens in our lives. Then we might reflect on God's will—what it means and how we imagine it. We may ask whether our images and ideas continue to make sense, including the claim that something that happens to us is God's will.

The Metaphor of God's Will

As I have suggested God's will is a metaphor, which is to say that the concept of God's will is metaphorical. To talk about God as having and exercising a will usually implies that God is a person and that God acts or exercises agency. Imagining God as a person is also a metaphor. This book is an exploration not only of metaphors for the person of God but also God's will. As we explore the nature and meaning of different metaphors for God, we will also be examining the ways that they describe God's will. We will consider such questions as: How does God act and exercise will? What kind of person is God? What are God's chief characteristics and attitudes? What does God most value? What happens to the metaphor of God's will if the divine is not imagined as person?

There is no one way to imagine God's will or to understand it. It is so rich and complex a metaphor that we have available to us an array of theological approaches, each of which conceives of God's will and how it works in a different way. The following chapters of this book survey this spectrum of approaches. No one of these approaches is *the* correct one. All can be found within the Christian tradition. There are persons who claim to find meaning and truth in each of these views of God's will. I will suggest that each has strengths and weaknesses. My own perspectives and preferences will be apparent in the process. I have already played my hand, so to speak, in the description of my vision of God as dynamic energy.

Each of the approaches to God's will also implies a particular understanding of God's power and how God uses power. This question of power, and God's power in particular, is key to understanding the different metaphors and approaches. Some theologians, who are paying more attention to the ways in which God's power is used for or against people, are unveiling the harm that can be generated by certain metaphors for God and the claims that are made about God's will.

In such instances God's will can be used as a weapon, especially if people are told that their lot in life is God's will or that rising up against those in power in contrary to what God's wants. In dramatic instances the church has preached to slaves and the poor that their condition is God's will for them. Prayers offered on their behalf reinforce that affirmation. Battered wives have been directed to be obedient to their husbands because to do otherwise is to go against God's will as stated in scripture.

Some theologians have questioned such conceptions of God's will and how they are used. However, for others, it is not enough to argue that God does not want the poor to remain poor or for wives to be battered. They have gone further to reimagine God's will as a positive and empowering force in the lives of people, including those who may have little access to power in the world.

These theologians, who are aware of the power of theological concepts, recognize that our ideas always reflect particular perspectives and contain bias. In this world theology functions as ideology. It undergirds political agendas. Theology does not only describe the world but shapes it. Theological ideas are not neutral or above the political fray. Nor is God. In that sense we need to consider whose side God is on and how that affects the way power is perceived and wielded. Theological ideas either reinforce cultural and political practices and structures or resist and change them. Therefore, it is all the more important to think about how theological concepts function and what they imply for our lives. Theology may be talk about God, but it is our lives that bear its impact.

Theology as Truth

The goal of theology is to tell the truth about God and the meaning and purpose of life. But how do we know what is true? Over the centuries Christian theologians have offered a variety of answers to that question. Most often those responses were based on a belief that God had revealed truth about God to us and our job was to try to understand what God had communicated. What God had revealed, God's revelation, was contained in scripture and in the teachings and traditions of the church. If we wanted to know what was true, we could turn to the Bible to find God's word or we could listen to what the church said. Some theologians also believed that we might be able to know God's truth through reason, in our ability to think and to imagine, and through God's created order, especially in the beauty and laws of nature.

More recently, theologians have suggested that human experience is a source for knowledge of God and that experience is, in fact, foundational even to Scripture and tradition. For these theologians scripture is the accumulated record and accepted, collective version of people's experiences of God. Others, especially those who view God as the more direct source of Scripture, would disagree. For them human experience has very little to do with God's truth. These different approaches to biblical truth have produced many debates about the meaning of scripture.

Even though theologians may differ in what they understand to be the sources of truth and their divine origin, most agree that there is a set body of truth, revealed by God. Theologians and believers are thus trying to apprehend this God-given truth and relate it to the lives of people today. Revealed truth remains constant, though the way it is understood and applied may change. For these theologians theology is the process of understanding the unchanging truth in different circumstances and settings. They may apply various criteria such as coherence of ideas, continuity with tradition and even connection with people's lives in order to assess and communicate truth, but ultimately they are seeking to make manifest what is already revealed.

I think differently about theology and truth. Truth is neither unchanging nor given. Nor is it propositional statements about the nature and actions of God. For me truth is practical: What is true is known by what it makes possible. Which is to say that I am concerned about the practical effects of theology.

Underlying this approach is a core assumption: What is of God is life-giving. What is not life-giving is not of God and, therefore, does not call for our allegiance. Something is life-giving if it empowers, enhances, and deepens the flourishing of creation, including human persons, and if it enables life to go on. This understanding of life does not automatically exclude death when it is a natural part of life and of finitude. Life may even include certain forms of violence within and among species. In other words, not everything that contributes to life ongoing is necessarily or always experienced as desirable.

These ideas about life and power will be explored further in the following chapters. What I would emphasize here is that if theology is ideology and if its use is a function of power, then how truth is defined and what it is used for and against become critically important. Truth is known and tested in the doing. It is manifest in the ideological uses of theology. For example, the Christian tradition maintains that God is the creator of everything that exists and that God affirms all that is created as having value and being good. In practice, however, Christians have asserted that some things are better than others and some people are better than others—a built-in hierarchy of value. As a result Christians have condoned discrimination and even violence against species and certain peoples. Given this history in what sense can Christians claim to believe in the value and goodness of all of creation?

Thus my approach to theology looks at the logic of certain ways of thinking and at what results are produced by such thinking and logic. Then I ask if these ideas, these ways of thinking, are ones I am able to hold as true because they are life-giving. The accrual of power by some against others and the use of violence to gain and maintain power over others are not life-giving. They are against life and so need not command our allegiance. In the end, all of the words in this book, all the words of every person who has ever claimed anything about God, would mean nothing if they did not engender life and hope.

Language for God

In the Christian tradition the metaphorical language used for God employs mostly male images and male pronouns. God is named as king and father not queen and mother. The pronoun used to refer to God is "he" even when the metaphor might not be gendered. For example, the line from psalms is translated: "God is our rock. He is our refuge." It is not translated: "God is our rock. It is our refuge."

The use of male language for God is neither accidental nor a choice of convenience. Male language reflects a world that privileges and values males. In such a word power and authority are associated with male-ness. Our religious language reinforces these associations.

The term "God" itself is generally understood as masculine. Female deities are referred to as Goddesses. Judaism and Christianity defined themselves over against other religions of the ancient world that honored Goddesses, so they fostered an aversion to female deities as representative of pagan polytheism. Neither Judaism nor Christianity view God and Goddess as equivalent terms, with the only difference being gender. They treat Goddesses as false deities. The one true deity is named God, and God is "he."

These historical and deeply ingrained dynamics produce a host of problems, especially when trying to develop more inclusive ways of imagining and talking about God. There are also very practical considerations. As an author how am I to refer to the divine in this book? What pronouns should I use, if any?

There are no easy or fully adequate answers to such questions. My accommodation is to continue to use the term "God," although I am well aware that it is most often used as a male term. I also use the term "the divine" to suggest the sacred life force of the universe without necessarily personifying it. I try to avoid the use of pronouns and when I cannot, I use the neuter (as I just did in the previous sentence) or alternate between "he" and "she."

In this book I also follow the language usage common to the metaphor for God that I am presenting. Therefore, in the next few chapters, when I describe the monarchical image of God or the patriarchal ones, I will continue to refer to God as "he." I will change to more inclusive usages or nongendered terms when considering the less exclusively male and nonpersonal images of God. Readers can then track the shifts in language use as reflective of changing theological and social perspectives and values.

I have covered much theoretical territory in this chapter and presented assumptions and underpinnings for what follows. Before going on, however, I want to remind the reader where I began: with a vision of the divine. I have returned to that moment of insight into nature of the divine—and of reality—again and again because I hold it as true. I hope readers will seek their truth, their vision of God, in and among and through what is offered in these pages. In the end, it is only by searching and sharing together that we can know the divine and experience life abundant.

2

LORD AND MASTER

GOD THE ALL POWERFUL MONARCH

"GOD HAS A PLAN FOR YOUR LIFE." "Whenever God closes a door, he opens a window. He knows what is coming, even if you don't." Expressions such as these are often used to assert that God is fully in charge and directing all of life. Everything is determined by God's will. When the young twin, Kayla, was killed in a horseback riding accident, her godmother attributed the death to God's desire for another angel for his choir. Some people believe that if they get a job offer, it is God's will. If they do not get the offer, that is also God's will. Still others think that whether their baby is born healthy or terribly deformed is determined by God's will. There are even those who believe that AIDS is God's will and punishment.

For these believers nothing is outside the scope of that will: Hurricane Katrina, a victorious battle against an enemy, the remission of a virulent cancer, the airline crash that kills a whole family, meeting one's life partner, passing a test, losing a child due to a drunk driver, and on and on. Whenever someone says, often in the face of tragedy, "It is God's will," she is implying that God controls and intends everything. Or when someone asserts, "There but for the grace of God, go I—or you," he is putting everything under God's charge.

It is easy to live with that judgment when good things happen. Why not believe that God wills for us to be offered the job we want or to find our dream house? After all, don't we pray for such things? We ask God to give us what we want or to make things turn out well for us. We pray for others as well, that God will be good to them and bestow on them what they need or want. The challenge comes when bad things happen and we wonder why. Why would God will Hurricane Katrina? Why would God allow a drunk driver to kill a young child? Why did God cure Jane's cancer but not Ellen's when we prayed with equal earnestness for them both?

We may well ask such questions, no matter how we understand God's will. When we assert that God is in total control, however, we need to be able to explain, or accept as unexplainable, the things that seem to challenge that control. If God is so powerful, why not cure both Jane and Ellen? Why not cure everyone? Those who favor this metaphor for God answer such questions by asserting God's power all the more.

God the Monarch

The God of this metaphor is a monarch, a divine monarch. He is addressed most often as lord. He is also called king and judge, master and warrior. He is viewed as powerful and mighty, as well as majestic and full of splendor.

Democracy may now be the favored form of government, but for many centuries, indeed for most of recorded history, nations, empires, and tribes were ruled by a king or emperor or tribal chief. Even if there were a ruling body related to the monarch, such as princes or a tribal council, power was held primarily by one person, most often male.

In such a world the monarch rules absolutely. Everyone and everything are subordinate to him. They have to obey his will. They exist to serve him. Indeed, their very lives are dependent on him. In the ancient Near East, where Judaism and Christianity were birthed and grew, oriental potentates presided over kingdoms and empires. They commanded obedience and deference. All power and privilege was theirs, to mete out to others as they chose.

We can see vestiges of this monarchical model in corporate America. In terms we know from the corporate world, a monarch is like the "chief executive officer" or the "chairman of the board." Most workers, except for those who are part of a union or have a binding contract, are "at will" employees. This means they can be fired, laid off, or let go at the will of their employer.

We may have also heard the phrase: "I serve at the pleasure of the President." Those who work for the president of the United States or other chief officers only have authority or position due to the desire or pleasure of the executive. That pleasure can be withdrawn at any point and then they are out of a job.

From these vestiges of monarchical privilege, we are able to get a taste of the immense power someone in such a position might have. Imagine increasing that power and privilege many times over, so that the monarch has control not only over someone's employment but also his or her very life. That monarch can order someone killed or issue a decree affecting the lives of thousands of people without being held accountable. The monarch's will rules the realm. In recent history we have witnessed such uses of power by ruling dictators such as Saddam Hussein in Iraq or Idi Amin in Uganda.

We may well recoil from such absolute and arbitrary power, especially when it is used to cause harm and to oppress. Many a revolution has been born in resistance to abuses by monarchs. For such revolutionaries the monarch has become an autocrat, a dictator, and a tyrant.

Even though, in the last several centuries, one revolutionary movement after another has challenged the rule and power of autocrats, the metaphor of God as a monarch has remained strong. In democratic societies leaders pay attention to the will of the people and even hear slogans such as "power to the people," but God is still often seen as an absolute ruler with total power. His will is the one that counts.

God as lord is often pictured as seated upon a throne, ruling all and meting out justice. He reigns from above, over a tiered and hierarchical universe. Any monarch needs a court and God is no exception, so throngs of angels and archangels, the heavenly hosts surround the lord. This court may also include the chosen ones whom the lord has allowed into his presence, that is, those who enjoy heaven, an eternal paradise.

In Christian depictions the risen Christ often accompanies God the monarch. The titles of lord and master apply to Jesus Christ as well. Sometimes Christ is shown as seated on the right hand of God, or he may occupy the throne alone, adorned with the signs of monarchy and kingship: scepter and orb, crown and robe. Over the main entrance of many a cathedral built in the Middle Ages is a scene of the last judgment, with Christ in the middle, reigning from above and presiding over the judgment of all who would seek to enter heaven.

God the monarch's primary attributes include power and might, as well as majesty and splendor. Hymns depict this God and offer him praise, whether as first or second person of the Trinity.

> Praise, my soul, the King of heaven;
> to his feet thy tribute bring;
> ransomed, healed, restored, forgiven,
> evermore his praises sing. . . .

> God, my King, thy might confessing,
> ever will I bless thy Name;
> day by day thy throne addressing,
> still will I thy praise proclaim. . . .

> All hail the power of Jesus' Name!
> Let angels prostrate fall;
> bring forth the royal diadem,
> and crown him Lord of all!

God in the Superlative

God the monarch is not just powerful and mighty, he is *all* powerful and almighty. Since God is beyond compare, whatever characterizes him is necessarily in the superlative mode. God cannot simply be powerful or comparatively more powerful. He must be the most powerful. Ultimately, all power is his.

This is what the term *omnipotent*, used in reference to God, means. The other "omni" attributes of God are *omnipresent* and *omniscient*. *Omnia* is the Latin term for "all." So God is all powerful, all present, and all knowing. Even though presence and knowing are distinct attributes, the point of all the "omnis" is to affirm God's power. God is everywhere, always. God knows everything. Therefore, there is nowhere God is not and nothing that God does not know, throughout time and eternity. God is not limited or localized in any way.

God's will functions in the superlative mode as well. Because God is all powerful, all present, and all knowing, God's will is in total control, all directing and all determining. God's will is absolute, not subject to influence or limitation. God is able to do whatever God wants. Nor does God have to answer to anyone or anything for his actions. God is not accountable other than to himself.

In part this accountability to himself means that God would not contradict himself; that is, God would not do something that is contrary to his attributes and his nature. For example, God would not will evil, since God is good and evil is other than or not part of God.

God's will is also supreme. There is nothing beyond it. Anything other or less would be a compromise of God's power, if not the very nature of God. Thus, God's will is omnipotent, able to do and accomplish whatever it chooses.

The Scope of God's Will

What does God will? What does God intend, control, and determine? These are key questions that may occupy those who favor this metaphor for God. The answer is often that all of life, and what happens in it, is already designed and laid out by God.

A favorite Bible verse cited in support of this view of God's will comes from the opening verses of Jeremiah: "Before I formed you in the womb I knew you, and before your were born I consecrated you; I appointed you a prophet to the nations" (1:5). These words suggest that

Jeremiah's vocation as prophet was determined by God before his birth. In subsequent verses, when Jeremiah protests that he is not able to do as God asks, God assures him that God will be with Jeremiah, guiding and directing him. God will provide him with what he needs to do God's bidding.

If God has already determined the course of our lives, then our job is to discern God's will and then obey it or fulfill it. Depending on how much of our lives we understand as scripted by God, we will view the task of discernment and obedience in different ways.

Some believe that plan is fully detailed. Everything that happens in a person's life has been determined and orchestrated by God, often before birth. There are no accidents. If a child is killed in a car crash, that is God's will. God has determined what occupation each of us will have and who our life partner will be or not be. Nothing is open ended. Nothing is "to be determined." We cannot see the plan as a whole, but it is there, all of it, in the mind of God.

Within this perspective the process of discernment may be fraught with anxiety, as there is only one right choice to be made. Alternatively, people may feel comforted by the perspective that whatever happens, God is in charge.

Others believe that God's will is in charge, although God allows more of a role for human will and decision making. God still sets the direction of our lives and has particular intentions for how to live those lives, but he leaves the details more up to us. For example, some believe that God's wills people to marry, have children, and live in families, but God does not choose specific life partners. God does not determine that Bill and only Bill should be Mary's husband; therefore, if Mary marries Paul, she is not opposing God's will. Discernment then becomes a process of determining what is the best fit for God's direction in our lives.

Another way to imagine the difference between these two approaches is to think of God as a manager. In the first view God is a total micromanager. God is "hands on" and involved in every phase of the process. In the second view God is still a manager who oversees everyone's life and makes sure everything goes as planned, but God delegates those decisions that do not affect the overall direction and outcome.

These "plans" that determine the details of our lives as well as their outcome have been in place from the beginning. Such plans include not only what happens to us in this life but also beyond this life. Predestination means that God decides who will be saved and who will not, that is, who will have eternal life. God wills and destines persons for such salvation. No one can be saved without God's determining will. Predestination is about God the monarch exercising his right over the life and death of his subjects.

There are a number of approaches among those Christians who hold to a doctrine of predestination as to its meaning and scope. For example, does God only save some or will God save everyone? Those who adhere to a concept of "limited atonement" believe that only some are saved, the elect whom God has chosen to save. But then how are people to know if they are chosen? Some theologians argue no one will know until the end of time. Others suggest that those who have accepted Christ as their savior or those who have found favor in God's eyes as evidenced by their lives will be saved.

What happens to those not chosen, not saved? Some theologians propose that those not chosen are more or less overlooked. Still others argue that God determines everyone's future, even condemning souls to eternal damnation. This is what double predestination means: that God both saves and condemns. Single predestination means that God saves some but leaves the rest aside, on their own, so to speak.

Yet another approach to the question of whom God wills to save proposes that God's will is for universal salvation, which means either that the possibility for salvation is available to everyone or that ultimately God will save everyone. This is a more expansive and inclusive view of God's will that is often opposed by those who believe in single or double predestination. Historically, *Arminianism*, named after Jacobus Arminius, who preached that God's saving will was intended for all, represented this more open view in opposition to Calvinists, many of whom professed double predestination.

Arminians stopped short of believing that God will save everyone. "Universalists" deem God's will as even more inclusive: God's saving will is universal, extending to all. Not surprisingly, such universalists have been opposed by those who believe in a more limited scope for God's saving will.

Ironically, a key concern for both sides in this opposition is God's power. The doctrine of double predestination is about affirming God's power as absolute and totally in control. Belief in universal salvation, or the possibility of it, is also an affirmation of God's power and what it is able to accomplish. Both predestination and universalism affirm God's freedom to do whatever God wills to do.

Freedom and Chance

One could well ask, if God has all this power, why does he not save everyone or prevent harm? This question leads to others, such as: granted God is all powerful, but how much of that power does God wield? Or, what is the meaning of God's freedom, especially as a function of power? And what is the relation of God's freedom to human freedom?

Freedom is related to will. One way to define freedom is the ability to do what one wills to do, to act without restraint or necessity. God wills freely, which is to say that God's will is not constrained in any way. God's freedom insures that God's will is effective. It is able to accomplish what it intends.

God the monarch's freedom also means that he does not have to will anything. God is not required to do anything. He is under no obligation. Again in the superlative mode, God the monarch is absolutely free.

Such freedom means there is no necessity in God. One of the traditional attributes of God, aseity, reflects this view of God. Aseity means that God exists in and of himself. He is a being unto himself. He does not need anything beyond himself.

Such need leads to necessity, which, in turn, conditions or restrains actions. For example, when we say, "We are not free to go out tonight, we have to take care of the children," we are pointing to a constraint on our freedom, a need—to attend to children—that limits our ability to do whatever we want.

God's aseity is meant to protect him from such constraint and limitation and to guarantee that anything God does is a totally free act. God did not need to create the universe. Nor did he need anything to do so, which is to say that God created *ex nihilo*, out of nothing. Neither does God have to save anyone or anything. However, because God has both created and saved, there is abundant evidence of God's freedom to accomplish what God wills.

Even though absolute freedom would seem to be compatible with open possibilities and room for chance, the omnipotent, omniscient, and omnipresent God leaves nothing to chance. God's all determining will banishes chance and accident from the universe. God controls everything. In that way God's freedom seems to impose necessity on everyone and everything else.

Are then human beings free? If God's will is all determining, what freedom do we human beings have in relation to God and to what happens in our lives?

We have already encountered one potential answer to that question: God sets out the overall plan for our lives, but we still have choices to make. Within the plan we have say over a variety of decisions. A crude example might be that God determines that we will live in a house outside Milwaukee, but we get to decide what color the walls will be painted, what flowers get planted, and what style of furniture we use.

Another answer to that question is that the freedom we have is to disobey God or turn away from God but not to choose God. This is the answer given by the Augustinian doctrine of original sin.

Sin and Grace

According to St. Augustine, God, in creation, willed for human beings to be free and to have free will because this was better and more fitting than creating them without freedom. God directed the first human beings, Adam and Eve, to use their free will to obey God. Instead, Adam and Eve disobeyed God. This misuse of their freedom resulted in its loss. For St. Augustine this meant that human beings no longer had the ability, on their own, to choose the good, to do the right thing, and to be obedient.

As a result of the disobedience of the first human beings, all of humanity was subjected to sin. Sin had power over everyone. Human beings no longer had the capacity or freedom to live as God created them to live. Sin distorted their wills so they were unable to act as intended.

In order to fulfill his creating and ordaining will, God the almighty intervened, through the person of Jesus Christ, to free enslaved humanity and make God's grace available to those to whom God chooses to give grace. Sinful human beings need grace to choose the good and to be saved. Without it they remain lost and captive to sin.

Grace is a free gift from God, undeserved because of disobedience and sin. God does not have to offer grace to everyone or anyone. Those who do not receive God's grace cannot be saved and so only those whom God chooses to save are offered grace.

Later Calvinist theologians went even further to suggest that those who are given God's grace cannot refuse it. In that sense they are necessarily saved. This idea, known as irresistible grace, again confirms God's freedom, power, and will over against human freedom, power, and will.

This way of thinking about grace may seem harsh to our modern sensibilities. The idea that all of humanity is forever affected by a single disobedience, even if the Genesis story is understood as myth, may seem farfetched. These ideas persist, however, in much Christian thinking not only about sin and grace but about the nature of God as monarch.

God's Goodness and Love

Clearly, God as lord and master is supremely powerful, but how are we to understand this absolute monarch as good or loving? This God is to be revered and feared. He inspires awe and perhaps even terror. What does it mean to love such a God or for him to love us?

It may be challenging to talk about love and goodness in the face of behavior that in someone else we might label tyrannical. If God can will the lives of all, some to live and others to die, then how is that different from what a tyrant might do? If God is absolutely free, then he is not accountable for what he does. Should such seemingly arbitrary behavior be called good, let alone loving?

The way God as lord and master expresses power is through control and domination (the derivation of which is the Latin word, *dominus*, which means master or lord). Such expressions of power do not fit easily with what we think of as goodness or love. How then are we to understand or define those attributes of God? What explanation might we offer for all the terrible things that happen that are attributed to God's will?

These questions are not new ones. Over the centuries a variety of answers have been developed. One long standing response to such questions, perhaps the most common one, argues that there is no explanation. God is a mystery; God's actions are mysterious. God the supreme sovereign is so transcendent, so categorically different and other than us, that we, with our limited capacities, cannot understand what God does or why. After all, we are not omnipotent, omnipresent, nor omniscient, so we cannot presume to know or see or act as God does.

The biblical passage often cited to indicate this difference is Isaiah 55:8-9:

> For my thoughts are not your thoughts,
> nor are your ways my ways, says the Lord.
> For as the heavens are higher than the earth,
> so are my ways higher than your ways
> and my thoughts than your thoughts.

These verses, along with Paul's image of seeing now through a mirror dimly but then face to face (1 Cor. 13:12), convey the idea that with our limited perspective and knowledge, who are we to question God's actions that we cannot understand.

Isaiah 55 continues, in the next two verses, to emphasize the effectiveness of God's power:

> For as rain and snow come down from heaven,
> and do not return there until they have watered the earth,
> making it bring forth and sprout,
> giving seed to the sower and bread to the eater,
> so shall my word be that goes forth from my mouth;
> it shall not return to me empty,

but it shall accomplish that which I purpose,
and succeed in the thing for which I sent it.

God is in charge and will prevail. Who are we to question him? Further, God does not need to explain his actions to us, let alone offer any justification for them. It is we who are to obey God, not God who needs to answer to us in any way. We need to have faith that God is good and true to his promises to us.

Another set of responses to questions about God's goodness emphasizes God's justice. God makes sure that justice prevails. That is the measure of his goodness. God may be a stern judge, but a fair one. God's justice may even be a terrible thing as reflected in the familiar words of the *Battle Hymn of the Republic*:

Mine eyes have seen the glory of the coming of the Lord;
He is trampling out the vintage where the grapes of wrath are
    stored;
He hath loosed the fateful lightning of His terrible swift sword;
His truth is marching on.
Glory! Glory! Hallelujah! Glory! Glory! Hallelujah!
Glory! Glory! Hallelujah! His truth is marching on. . . .

He has sounded forth the trumpet that shall never call retreat;
He is sifting out the hearts of men before His judgment seat;
Oh, be swift, my soul, to answer Him! Be jubilant, my feet;
Our God is marching on.

In the triumphalism of this hymn, we hear that God's truth and justice will prevail and those who can withstand God's judgment have nothing to fear. In fact, they are joyous at God's victory and their deliverance.

Because God's justice is always on the side of what is true and right and good, proponents of this perspective would suggest that it is terrible only for those who find themselves opposed to it. God's will is for justice, which in turn is executed through God's victory over evil and through final judgment. Goodness and justice are one. God's love is manifest through God's justice.

Yet another response to questions about the goodness of God's will argues that we human beings have lost all to sin and are undeserving of anything from God. God's offer of grace, however limited it may be, is then a supreme act of love and graciousness on God's part. Given that such grace cost God the death of his Son, God's love is an even greater act and gift. We ought only respond to it with gratitude and humility.

Those who know God's grace, especially those who feel rescued from the weight of their sins, attest mightily to the loving goodness of God. Such loving goodness is most often expressed and experienced as forgiveness. As many a redeemed sinner would testify, the availability of forgiveness is witness to the goodness and love of God. There is no doubt in their minds about God's care.

God as Liberator

However we might understand God's goodness and love, God as lord and master remains a sovereign, reigning over all, determining people's lives and willing what happens to them. These images of God are embedded throughout the worship and hymnody of many Christian churches. God is ever being addressed as almighty and as king of glory. Prayers to God declare "your will be done." Preachers proclaim God as the one directing our lives. Depictions of God as an absolute monarch, regal and majestic, as well as a mighty warrior, victorious in battle, have filled the prayers, music, art, and literature of churches for centuries.

So much of this imagery for God comes from social and cultural contexts vastly different from ours today. We do not live in kingdoms and empires ruled by kings and emperors. Our sensibilities are not those of imperial courts. We do not bow to kings; we rarely bow to anyone. Yet this imagery persists.

Sometimes it is adapted to contemporary perspectives, needs, and sensibilities. Such variations tend to forego the regal imagery but maintain the sovereignty of God. They assert God's power and might, but render God's power as more accountable. Although God remains in control and in charge, he metes out justice in a way that is more responsive to human need. Indeed God's just power challenges and confounds injustice in the world.

For example, in liberation theology, especially as first expressed in a South American context, the image of God as sovereign, ruler, and victor becomes God as liberator. God is still powerful, powerful enough to oppose those in power on earth, including despots. Indeed, God as liberator is the champion of those who suffer and are oppressed in this world. God remains all powerful, but God uses his power in a particular way, on behalf of those who are powerless. Affirmation of God's power becomes a judgment against the power of their oppressors and a hope for transformation of the conditions of the oppressed.

Liberation theologians who profess this view of God's power argue that God has made a preferential option for the poor and the oppressed. God is on their side, which means the powerless of the world are now empowered by God. The greatest power is *with them*. Drawing, for example, on the story of the Exodus, these theologians point out that God prevails against the powerful Pharaoh on behalf of the enslaved Israelites. African American theologians, along with colonized peoples throughout the world, have also drawn upon the Exodus story to claim God's promise and power of deliverance for them.

Many of these theologians, writing from the perspectives of the oppressed and downtrodden, believe that the God who works on behalf of the poor and oppressed will be victorious. In the end, the evil, harmful powers of the world will be defeated. God's good power will triumph and all those who have suffered wrong will be vindicated and liberated.

Some view liberation not as political freedom, but as spiritual and personal transformation. God's power is able to free those held in bondage because of social systems, interpersonal violence, and abuse, addictions, or debilitating fears. God will be victorious against such powers and forces. God will free those held captive.

Whether the battle is on earth or in the cosmos, in our psyches or in our homes, God the liberator is able to defeat the forces of evil. He is a mighty warrior, wielding great power to make right what has been wronged and to restore what has been lost. God's will is able to prevail against all that might oppose it. God exercises judgment or might to make sure that goodness wins out.

God as Magician

Another variation on this metaphor of the all powerful God is thinking of God as a magician, able to pull things out of hat. Those who see God in this way subscribe to a form of magical thinking. They pray to God to fulfill their wishes and expect God to come through for them. God is there to respond to and fulfill human needs.

People have always asked God, in prayer, for what they want. When they do so they are appealing to God's power and God's ability to be in charge. When people pray to the magician God, their expectation is that God will work magic for them, for *them*.

Even though God the magician is viewed as all powerful, able to do whatever people wish for, magical thinking implies that God's will can be manipulated to respond to human desires, human will. God exists to meet human needs. God's power is subject to human desire.

In the anthropocentric, if not narcissistic, world of modernity and postmodernity, this is a popular perspective. Many expect God to fulfill their needs and wants, magically. If God is so powerful, then he can use his power to answer their prayers and give them what they want and need.

Popular preachers sometimes advocate this thinking by making promises about what God will do and making God out to be a personal miracle worker. Drawing on biblical miracles these preachers portray God as someone who will provide manna from heaven, work instant cures, and deliver plagues on enemies. People then expect God to provide money for the electric bill or instant healing of chronic illness.

People who believe in this approach to God may also imagine God as a wizard, such as in *The Wizard of Oz*. He is an all powerful and demanding being, hidden from direct access. Yet it is he whom we must encounter in order to get what we need. God's ways of working are other than human ways, but his power is unquestionable. He is able to defy the laws of nature and do what we lowly mortals can only imagine as magic.

Prayer and Worship of the Lord and Master

God the all powerful monarch commands and demands worship. The point of such worship is to affirm God's power and greatness. It is to extol who God is and what God is able to do, which are always in contrast to who we are and how little we are able to do. Worship of God includes the admission that human beings lack power and so are utterly dependent on God. All prayers come to the same conclusion: "Your will be done, O Lord, for yours is the greatness and the power and the majesty."

For those who relate to this metaphor for God, this affirmation is freeing and empowering. It releases them from carrying their burdens alone. It promises them that someone else, upon whom they may rely, is in charge. They are not vulnerable to chance and chaos. Ultimately, evil will be defeated and the powers of this world put in their place.

Such assurances surely evoke praise, the primary mode of prayer to God the monarch. Christian worship services always include, and very often begin with, praise. In prayers and hymns worshipers tell God how wonderful, glorious, and powerful he is and express awe and gratitude. They recognize who God is, in all his glory, and what God has done: "Blessed are you, Almighty King of the universe, who has brought us to this day and granted us life."

There is a type of flattery in such praise, especially when affirmations about how wonderful and powerful God is are contrasted with our own helplessness and sinfulness. For example, a typical prayer offered to God the monarch might be: "Even though we are unworthy to offer you any praise, O Lord, yet you are merciful and slow to anger, you hear our prayers and are gracious toward us."

The other main form of prayer directed toward God the monarch is petition. In prayers of petition we ask God for things, for what we want and need, for ourselves, for others, and for the world. Petition is probably the most common form of prayer to God, and we will revisit it in succeeding chapters. In this metaphor for God, however, those who pray not only petition God for what they need and want, but they also plead with God. Since God is totally is charge, and God's will rules and determines all, prayers involve such an element of plea.

In a court of law, petitioners, represented by lawyers, plead a case to the judge. They present arguments and ask the judge (or jury) to be fair or merciful. Expressions such as "throwing oneself on the mercy of the court" reflect this dynamic of pleading. In imperial courts, subjects would implore the monarch to fulfill their petitions. They would bring their claims, whether they were for land or for release from some obligation or for settling a dispute, before the monarch who would then issue rulings and judgments.

Such petitioning and pleading reflect the truth that God as monarch and judge is the one with the power and authority to act, determine and decree. All we can do is ask, humbly. We cannot demand or even expect anything other than what God wills and gives. We may trust in God's fairness and mercy, but we have no right, no position of power or privilege of our own from which to demand anything from God.

Because, as testified to in Scripture, God has made certain promises, such as in the covenant with Israel or through the life, death, and resurrection of Jesus, petitioning and pleading with God may involve recalling these promises. Implicit in appeals to God's mercy is a type of reminder to God that he did indeed promise to be merciful.

Yet another form of prayer that fits this metaphor for God is confession, which includes contrition and penitence. In confession the penitent asks God for mercy and is prepared to accept the judgment of God. Kneeling, a bodily posture often associated with confession, is not only a penitential stance, but also one of obeisance, a sign of humility and submission.

Submission is at the center of prayer and worship to God the monarch. Worshipers are demonstrating through word and action and bodily posture that God is almighty and powerful. They are but his humble subjects, bowing before him and submitting to his will.

In the Armenian Apostolic Orthodox church in which I grew up, the priest's vestments were patterned on that of a regal monarch. Over his robes, the priest wore a long cape and a crown. Except for the white tunic underneath, the other vestments were fashioned from rich fabrics, with gold embroidery, reflective of imperial garments. With all this regalia, the priest reflected and represented God. He was considered holy and treated with reverence.

Holiness means otherness and connection with God. Whether such holiness is an attribute of the clergy or the church building or objects in the church, people and things that are holy are set aside, treated in special ways. They hold a particular power because they are considered to be closer to God. They reflect God's glory and majesty. Therefore, they are to be approached with reverence and treated with special care.

Protestant reformers, arguing that the access of the faithful to God did not require mediation by special persons or things, stripped away regal vestments and elaborate church furnishings. Protestantism, however, did not lessen God's power or the necessity of submission to God. Holiness was transferred to God's word and those who spoke God's word.

Recognition of the holiness of God's word might not require reverence in the form of bowing before the altar or sacred objects, but it does demand obedience and submission. In such churches, worshipers still bow their heads in prayer. They believe that God's word, as pronounced and as preached, reflects God's power and will. In the more biblically literalist forms of Protestantism, the Bible is word for word the expression of God's will. Its authority is absolute. The faithful are to adhere to it and obey it without question.

In the beginning and in the end, in all the churches that view God as an almighty ruler and monarch, omnipotent, omniscient, and omnipresent, God's will is the mark and measure of all that happens and all that the faithful are to be and do. "Your will be done" is the constant refrain of those faithful.

The Strengths of This Metaphor

A chief strength of this metaphor is affirmation of the power of God. God is almighty; God is in charge. Many people claim this as "blessed assurance," especially in times when evil seems to be winning out, when they are oppressed or in great need. In situations and times that people may feel powerless, the faith that there is a higher power, greater than themselves, can offer comfort, solace, and strength. Whether subject to a form of personal captivity, such as addiction, or political captivity, such as living under an oppressive regime or being the object of discrimination and terror, imagining God as more powerful than one's captors and oppressors can support survival and even the ability to produce change.

Related to this strength is affirmation of the otherness and transcendence of God. Because God is not like, and may well be opposed to, the things of this world, the power of God may function to put the powers of this world in their place. In that way the otherness of God stands in judgment against whatever might seek to claim ultimate power in this world or purport to be divine.

A view of God as all powerful may also provide secure footing in a world that would otherwise seem to be ruled by chance and chaos. In the affirmation that nothing that happens is by chance or even by accident, that everything is God's will, is the assurance that there is meaning and purpose to all of life. As meaning seeking creatures, we human beings want to hold on to a belief that life and all that happens in it has purpose. Especially in the face of great tragedy and harm, even if we cannot imagine and fathom the purpose, we may find solace in knowing that such purpose exists in the mind of God.

Another strength of this metaphor is just that reminder: our vision and knowledge is limited. We do not have God's perspective on things. Our evaluative judgments are based on partial knowledge. We do not see the whole picture and so cannot be sure that our perspectives, let alone judgments, are true. Therefore, if we desire to act wisely, we would refrain from absolute pronouncements and judgments.

The Limitations of This Metaphor

The metaphor of God the monarch does not reflect the world in which we live. For many of us our only knowledge of emperors and kings is through books and films. Our image of a monarch is Queen Elizabeth II, who is more a symbol of duty and ceremony than of power. The societies we inhabit value democracy and human rights and tend to oppose the wielding of arbitrary and absolute power. Such uses of power are associated with dictators and despots. In democratic societies power is distributed so that no one person or one body is all powerful. What then does it mean to attribute such power to God?

This question suggests a couple of other problems with this metaphor. A primary one is God's lack of accountability for his actions. If God is all powerful and in charge, should then God not be responsible for what happens? Such accountability, however, would mean that God has to answer for evil and the bad things that happen.

Because evil is always other than God and therefore God cannot be responsible for it, God's power ends up pitted against his goodness in a dualistic framework. If God is to be both good and powerful, then the bad things either cannot be really bad—they are for our own good somehow—or God has nothing to do with them.

This dualistic framework affects our relationship to God as well. Given that the proper response to God the monarch is obedience and submission, one cannot have a relationship with God that is open and free. In fact, those who do not submit to God are not on God's side and are therefore considered evil. So often those without power in the world have been given only those choices: submit or be considered bad. Obedience is the only acceptable "good" behavior. This logic has been not only problematic, but also harmful for those with less power, such as the oppressed and women.

The monarchical God more often than not supports the status quo of earthly power. God the monarch serves to conserve and confirm given power arrangements, which in turn may abuse those with less power. For example, God's power is reflected and carried by those who are considered closer to God or who speak for God, such as the church and its clergy. Clergy tend to function as minimonarchs who demand obedience and whose authority is absolute in ways that both discount the voices and experiences of others and also lend themselves to abuses of all sorts.

Further, God the monarch and warrior has served as an ally in campaigns of imperial expansion and colonization. This sword-wielding monarch made his power and might known against peoples around the globe, often in the name of civilization. He was depicted as the conquering hero, bringing enlightenment and redemption to those who would otherwise live in darkness and condemnation. Given that such redemption was so often imposed by force, it was more often a power play than a saving act.

Since this God is always pictured as male and white, a conquering hero or royal monarch, other ways of imagining God are excluded. In this way, too, the language and imagery used for God the monarch support the hierarchical and unjust structures in power. For example, opponents of the ordination of women consistently argue that women cannot image or represent God, which often means that women cannot hold authority.

The fundamental limitation of this metaphor, and one that runs through much of what I have already pointed out, is the definition of power as control and domination, as "power over." This is too narrow and even dangerous an understanding of power, as will become evident in later chapters. Such power renders other expressions of power as hidden, suspect, or illegitimate.

Power as domination tends to oppose change and to label it as bad, a threat to the established order. In an ever-changing world this is a problem, if for no other reason than it offers few resources for responding to change in any way but rejection. For those of us who value equality and the distribution and balance of power, it is also dangerous for anyone, even God, to hold power absolutely.

God the monarch is not, however, the only image of God as all powerful and commanding. A related metaphor is of God as patriarchal father, lord of his household. He is the subject of the next chapter.

3

FATHER KNOWS BEST

GOD THE PATRIARCH

Undoubtedly, the most commonly known metaphor for God is father. When people imagine God as an old man with a long white beard, they are often thinking of God as a father and as a patriarch. In the next few chapters I explore different ways in which this metaphor of God as father is imagined and developed. I also examine the characteristics of God that correspond to these different approaches. In this chapter, my focus is on God the father as a patriarch, the head and ruler of a hierarchical order. The next two chapters consider variations on this parental image that make God the father less patriarchal and more relational.

God the patriarch knows what is best for us. He directs our lives. His power is supreme. All else is subordinate to God. This image of a patriarchal God both manifests in and is mirrored by experiences of childhood in patriarchal families.

Patriarchal Families

"This is for your own good." Every parent, at some point, has probably said those words to a child. "This" may refer to any number of things.

A parent may be insisting that a child brush his teeth or keep to her bedtime. Perhaps the parent is limiting the amount of television a child may watch or signing the child up for summer school. It may even be the case that the parent is imposing a punishment for something the child did wrong or insisting that a sick child take a medicine he hates. In all these cases the parent is making a judgment about what is good and necessary for the child. The parent is also imposing his or her will on the child and indicating that the parental will takes precedence over the child's will and desires.

Parents also make sure that children follow through. They not only tell children to brush their teeth or turn off the television but check to see if they do so. Left on their own, few children, it is assumed, would do what is good for them: go to bed at the appropriate hour or eat healthy meals.

Children obey their parents and go along with parental direction because they believe their parents want what is best for them. They love their parents. They may also fear them. Sometimes they experience both feelings.

On some level children also sense a need for structure and order in their lives. Order helps them feel safe and secure and so they submit to adult control. Good parents provide the order and structure that allows children to feel they are being attended to well.

Children need, and so are dependent on, their parents or adult guardians. Without adults to take care of them, children would not have adequate food or shelter, love or care. Children who are deprived of these needs fail to thrive. Their lives are harmed, often forever.

Because of their dependence and need, children have less power in relationships with adults. This is not to say that children do not exert their wills. Parents, adult guardians, and babysitters have all had the experience of a child questioning their direction: "Why should I eat my broccoli?" "Why can't I stay up and watch more TV?" Just about every-one who has been challenged in those ways has, at some point, said: "Because I say so." And perhaps has added, "Because I'm the parent (or the adult or the babysitter)." The message is clear: Do as I say, because I am in charge and what I say goes. The adult's direction counts more than the child's objection or questioning. It is often at such moments that the adult may also say: "This is for your own good."

Because we live in a society and in families in which the voices of children are sometimes heard, adult "say so" is not absolute. How children feel and what children want do count. The needs of children are often (some would say too often, and others would say not often enough) given priority. Parents care deeply about their children and are responsive to them, including trying to answer their children's questions and give reasons for what they are asking their children to do.

There are also safeguards against absolute parental rule. Parents may know best, but their knowledge can be assessed and measured by how well they raise their children. Laws and government agencies exist to oversee such care. The state takes children away from parents if the children are neglected and harmed. Laws legislate against abuse and mandate that children receive an education. However well these laws and regulations work, the fact that they exist is a relatively recent social phenomenon.

It used to be that neither families nor society were so child-centered. Remember the old adage: Children are to be seen and not heard. Or even: Spare the rod and spoil the child. In other times and cultures, the focus of family life was not as much on the growth and development of the child, as on the needs of the parents or the family as a whole. Children's needs were thus subordinate and their wants irrelevant. The primary role of children was to be obedient.

Social attitudes toward children have often been determined by economic necessity. For example, in agricultural societies the contributions of all the members of a household are necessary for the economic well-being of the family. In such a society, if an able-bodied son chooses to do some other type of work, the life and even survival of the family is threatened. The needs of individual family members must then be subordinated to the common good of the family as an economic unit. That unit is ruled by the father, the patriarch.

In modern, industrial societies, not only have families become more child-centered, but the roles of fathers and mothers have been shifting and blending in the last several decades. Those roles are no longer as differentiated from one another as they once were. The *Father Knows Best* household, with the father going out to work and the mother staying home, taking care of the children, and deferring to his authority, is becoming a rarity. Both parents are now usually working, both are involved in nurturing and caring for, as well as directing and guiding, children. Fathers are present in delivery rooms. They are as likely to put children to bed when then come home as to admonish or punish them.

These changes are, however, recent and not necessarily widespread. In the 1950s family in which I grew up, my father would sometimes play with my brother and me, and he would reprimand and punish us, but he never changed a diaper or made us a meal. My parents owned a grocery store; our residence was in the same building. Even though my father was never more than a flight or two of stairs away and my mother worked in the store alongside my father, even though both contributed to our family's economic life, my father did not participate in either housework or childcare. He did, however, control the household, including its money, and he determined what I could and could not do. At my mother's insistence I had to ask my father for permission for such things as buying a new dress or visiting a friend. He was in charge of the family, including our social and economic life. He was the patriarch.

Patriarchal Households

In a patriarchal household the father figure is the head of the family. He has the power and the authority. He rules the family and everyone else is dependent on him. The father uses his power to regulate the life of the household. He rules directly or through others by dispensing power to them. Thus any power that others have is derived from him. These dynamics apply to all the ways in which power is manifest, whether it is economic power or personal authority.

For example, in my mother's generation and even in mine, when wives divorced or even when they were widowed, they found they did not qualify for credit cards in their own names because they had no credit history. All the financial transactions of the household had been in their husbands' names. In some societies women still cannot own or inherit property. Such realities render women economically dependent on men. Their husbands and fathers and even sons maintain control.

In such situations whatever power a woman has is derived from the male head of the household. When a mother says, "Your father won't be happy when he hears about this" or "Wait until your father gets home," she is not only deferring to her husband but indicating that her own authority to discipline her children is based on his. The subtext of such statements is: He left me in charge; he gave me authority.

In a patriarchal household the patriarch's will rules everyone and everything. It is not a democracy. Even if there are family meetings and vote taking, ultimately what the father says is determinative. His will is the one that matters. Family members are expected to obey that will. The patriarch doles out permission or denies it. He also maintains order through giving direction and punishing offenses. The will of the patriarch is correct, as well as commanding. Whatever he orders is for everyone else's good.

Such a patriarchal household order is based on the operating assumption that what is good for the head of the household is good for everyone else. The dynamics of the household are focused on the needs and wants of the patriarch. His desires, his requirements, his direction are what count. They take precedence. Dinner is served according to his schedule. He is offered food before anyone else. He commands the best seat in the house. The needs and wants of individual members of the household are given lower priority and are subordinated to his.

Maintaining the given order is paramount in such a household. Whatever disturbs that order and the patriarch at its head is understood to be a threat. Individual members participate in the good of the whole by staying in their place and carrying out their assigned roles and functions. They make sure dinner is prepared when the patriarch wants it and that no one else sits in his chair. He controls the remote for the television. No one spends money without his permission or makes a major decision without his approval.

Since the order of a patriarchal household is maintained by keeping everyone and everything else subordinate, that is, under orders, insubordination cannot be tolerated. Challenging one's place in the hierarchy or questioning the order itself is a form of insubordination. It is taken as an affront to the will of the patriarch, who knows best. Children are to obey, not question, their father's commands. Wives are to do their husband's bidding and meet his needs.

In turn the patriarch's job is to take care of the household by providing for it, as well as directing and commanding it. "He's a good provider" was strong praise to give a father in the 1950s and even today. Heads of households often measure their worth by how well they provide and how good a life they make possible for those who are in their charge and dependent on them. By fulfilling their obligation to provide for those in their charge, fathers maintain the patriarchal order.

That order affords not only organization but security and peace as well. Hierarchy, as a form of governance, structures the social group—whether it be the family or the society—by establishing rules, defining roles, and marking boundaries strictly. Hierarchical structures function to manage conflict and protect against chaos through ordering life on all levels and maintaining a single, central authority. Fathers adjudicate conflicts and maintain peace in the family, often by having the final say. Their word rules.

Such a structure may be comforting to family members, especially in times of uncertainty and change and conflict. As long as father knows best and is in charge, then there is protection against those things that disturb the order and even threaten life. Depending on the context, the words "wait until your father gets home" can offer comfort as well as threat.

God as Patriarch

God as patriarch is the ruler of the universe. Everything within that universe is part of God's household; it is all God's domain. God directs and controls all that is subordinate to him. Everything is subject to God's will.

The universe of the patriarchal God is hierarchical. The college professor, whom I cited in the first chapter, held such a view of God. She believed in a tiered universe with God as father positioned atop that hierarchy. Such a worldview was for her the nature of reality; it was not a metaphor but a given.

She is not alone in her view. Many people of faith, especially those in monotheistic religions who believe there is only one God, often view the universe of that God as hierarchical. Both Christianity and Judaism have traditionally understood God in patriarchal terms.

God as patriarch orders the universe and provides for it and for each of us. From atop the hierarchy God the father directs all beneath him. Hierarchy works from the top down. Everything has its place. Such placement is by design. It is God given. There is nothing arbitrary in God's ordering. Obedience to God and to those above in the hierarchy is a primary virtue. Such obedience means staying in one's God-given place and following orders and direction. Challenging the given order or one's place in it is contrary to God's will.

We encounter this God and this view of creation at the very first, in the creation stories of the book of Genesis. In Genesis we read that not only does God create the universe and everything in it, but God does so in a particular way. There is a given order. Human beings are placed at the top of the earthly order and, therefore, they have dominion over all the rest of creation. There has been much discussion and debate over the centuries, and still today, about the meaning of such dominion: Does the rest of creation exist to serve human needs and wants, or are human beings meant to be caretakers? Regardless of whether the emphasis is on control over or responsibility for, the rest of creation remains somehow subordinated to human life.

The hierarchical structure built into creation extends to the relationship of men and women, as established with Adam and Eve. Again, there continues to be much discussion and dispute about what the intended relationship of Adam and Eve, as described in the creation narrative, was to be. However we may understand that story today, there is no doubt that for much of Christian history, Eve was believed to have been formed from Adam's rib and thus created second or after Adam. This reading of the story has been used to define women as subordinate to men, wives as subject to husbands. Thus the relationship of men and women is hierarchical. It was established as such in God's good creation.

The Genesis story also tells us that God provided for all in the garden of Eden. There was abundance. Everything that God created was, in that way, under God's care. The goodness of creation suggests that there was peace as well as abundance. Eden remained a paradise as long as everything and everyone fulfilled their God ordained purpose.

Thus, God's intent in creation was for human beings to live in an ordered relationship of obedience to God. From the very first God issued a command that Adam and Eve were not to eat of the fruit of the tree in the middle of the garden. As the familiar story goes, these first humans disobeyed this command, ate the fruit of that tree, and then were chastised and punished by God. Their punishment included exile from the garden. They no longer could claim a place in the peaceful existence of paradise.

Within this familiar Genesis story of creation and fall, the various roles of the patriarchal father are narrated: he creates, orders, rules, directs, provides, judges, chastises and punishes, and even exercises mercy. God's will is operating through each of these roles. Whatever God is doing, the patriarchal will is being manifest. That will is the instrument of God's action.

God Creates and Orders

Creation is through God's will. In the book of Genesis, the language used to describe God's act of creation refers to word and speech. God creates through a speech act. God said let there be light, and there was light. The word of God is able to create life. We encounter this affirmation again in the story of the conception and birth of Jesus Christ, whom the Gospel of John refers to as the Word. In the story of the Annunciation, Mary conceives in a conversation with the archangel Gabriel. Many an artist's portrayal of the annunciation shows the Word, carried by breath or by the Holy Spirit, depicted as a bird, issuing forth from the mouth of God and entering the womb of Mary.

God's will orders what God has made and rules it. Whatever hierarchical structure is present in creation, God intended it to be there. God created the world that way on purpose. Thus, it is God's will that humans have dominion over creation. It is also God's will that men and women marry and that wives be subject to their husbands.

Many argue that it is God's will that only men and women marry. For them, homosexual relationships are against God's will. They are outside of God's intended order. Such relationships are viewed as unnatural—that is, contrary to the order of creation. This perspective assumes that the Genesis story, as it has commonly been interpreted, defines God's will for human relationships, including sexual relationships, by ordering them in set ways.

God created woman and man for each other, to be fruitful and multiply. Any other expressions of sexuality are against God's will. For example, the Roman Catholic Church's stance against birth control is based on the idea that God's intent in creation is that sexual activity be for the purpose of procreation. Having sex without the possibility of procreating, which would be the case if a couple were using birth control or if the couple were of the same gender, is thus against God's will.

God's order determines the right way to live and the ends or purposes for which we strive in life. Obedience to God means living in such a way that we fulfill those purposes, or at least do not interfere with or negate them.

God Directs and Controls

God the patriarch not only orders but also directs and controls through his will. God's will is the source of everything that happens. God is in charge; nothing escapes God's notice. The patriarchal God is not an uninvolved father. He is fully engaged with all of creation.

God the patriarch is as powerful and all knowing and omnipresent as God the monarch, and his will is as absolute. However, God as father uses his power and knowledge somewhat differently. God the patriarch directs in and through the hierarchical structure that he established. In that way God delegates authority and disperses power to some degree, but only as long as the authority and power stay within the order that God created.

Ultimately, however, everything that happens is somehow directed by God's will. The medieval theologian, Thomas Aquinas, wrote of primary and secondary causes when discussing God's will. God's direct willing is the primary cause, but God acts through secondary causes, which may be human actions. For example, if a doctor's skill in an operation saves someone's life, that doctor is the secondary cause of God's will for that person being realized. The doctor is not simply a puppet, without free will or the ability to act on her own. God is not moving the surgeon's hands or telling her what to do. However, God is the primary cause of her skill and of the application of that skill to saving this person's life.

When we pray and submit a decision or action to God's will, we acknowledge God's authority and power. At the same time, even when we say, in prayer, "your will be done," we are not necessarily giving up our own responsibility or active engagement. We still make sure we do our best in the situation. When athletes kneel in prayer or make the sign of the cross, they are asking, crediting, and thanking God, so to speak, for the homerun or the touchdown. But that does not mean they do not train as hard as they can or use every skill they have. Because God gave us the talents, abilities, and skills we possess, they are valuable gifts to be nurtured and tended, even while we thank God for them.

In the hierarchical structure of the patriarchal God, all originates from and returns to the source at the top. Ultimately, the power and the credit reside there. God's will is the explanation for everything because God is directing all to its proper ends.

God's Providence

God's will also provides. In the Genesis story we read that everything that human beings and that the rest of creation need was given to them, in abundance, by God. God the patriarch is thus a good provider. This belief is affirmed again and again in the biblical story. For example, when the Israelites were wandering in the desert and fearing that they would perish, God provided manna from heaven for them to eat.

God's providential care is at the core of the biblical story. Whether in the pleas of the psalmist or the teachings of Jesus, the belief that God answers prayers and gives us what we need is attested to again and again. Faith is often defined as such belief in the constancy and sufficiency of God's providence. Sayings, such as "God will never give you more that you can handle" or "God may not come when you want him, but he will always be on time," testify to the belief that God is in charge and that God's care is always active, even in the most trying and difficult of circumstances.

It is often in such moments of difficulty or acute suffering that the faithful wonder about the providence of the patriarchal God. Their questioning often takes form of asking *why?*—Why did my young child have to die? Why would God send an earthquake that kills thousands of people?

How can we reconcile such events with the providence of God, with God's promise of care and sustenance? The answer we receive within this metaphor for God affirms that God the father is powerful and good: that father knows best and that what God is doing is ultimately for our own good. In this way, even when that "good" is difficult to imagine or when any good outcome could not, it seems, justify the nature and extent of the injury, God's will is affirmed. Even in the case of massive natural disasters, such as an earthquake or a hurricane, God's will is accepted. When people offer responses in the face of disaster and tragedy such as "God will bring a greater good out of the tragedy" or "God has an ultimate purpose that we cannot discern," they are testifying to the power and goodness of God. These responses are variations of the logic of the patriarchal system: God is in control. God knows best. So, ultimately, this is all for the good, for your good.

Thus God's providence is at work, no matter what evidence there may be to the contrary. God's providential care remains steadfast, even if cannot be discerned. God is a good provider.

God Judges and Punishes

God the father is a strict disciplinarian. God's care is not without judgment. God the patriarch is also God the judge. Many of us imagine God in this way, as the one who judges us. He is the old man with the white beard who sits on a throne of justice where he weighs our lives on his scales of justice. God pronounces judgment: whether we will be eternally rewarded or punished.

God as judge evokes our fear. We obey him out of fear. We live our lives in anticipation of the moment of judgment to come. Just as a mother's threat—wait until your father gets home—is meant to frighten children into behaving better, the prospect of a final judgment casts it shadow upon our behavior throughout our lives.

God as judge is all knowing and all powerful. When Adam and Eve sinned by eating the forbidden fruit, God was aware of it. He called them to account for their disobedience and passed judgment on them for it. That judgment included a punishment: They were banished from paradise. As a result, they were to experience pain and suffering. Eve would have great pain in childbirth and she would be subordinate to Adam. Adam would have to toil and sweat to provide for himself and his family.

Throughout the biblical story we find narratives and images of God as judge and as the one who assigns punishments. When God was unhappy with the corruption and violence he saw on earth, he sent a flood to destroy all but Noah, his family, and the inhabitants of the ark. When the people of Israel disobeyed God's command by building and worshipping a golden calf, God was so angry that Moses had to implore God not to kill them all. Moses intervened, as a mother often does in a patriarchal household, to soften and turn aside the wrath of the father. Even though God backed down from slaying the people in that moment, he sent a plague upon them and promised punishment for sin.

God's judgment and chastisement is also a prominent feature of the prophetic writings in the Bible. The prophets were called and sent by God to pronounce judgment on the people of Israel because Israel had strayed from God's ways. Through their harsh words of condemnation, the prophets communicated the wrath of God. Their intent was to chastise and correct the people. God's wrath is not arbitrary; it is a purposeful method of judgment. It communicates God's will. God's punishment follows upon God's wrath and condemnation. The prophets pronounced that when Israel was invaded and the people of Israel sent into exile in

Babylon, God was punishing Israel for its apostasy and wrongdoing, for its failure to live within the covenant promises.

In Christianity God's judgment is manifest not only in this life but finally in the last judgment. Jesus, in the Gospels, preached such judgment. He employed vivid imagery, such as the wrath of God, and parables about who would find favor with God and who would not. God's will is pronounced in and through judgment and assignment to heaven or hell. God's wrath is often measured by the intensity of the fires of hell.

Despite the fear that the anticipation of judgment and punishment instills in believers, they still maintain that God the father knows best. Whatever punishment they are given, it is their due. The chastising rod of God's discipline is meant for their own good. God's justice is expressed through judgment and punishment. The proper relationship to God is one of obedience.

God Is Merciful

God's judgment is tempered by God's mercy. In the Hebrew scripture God's justice and mercy are poles of God's will for Israel. The prophets not only pronounced God's wrath and chastisement, but also God's compassion. They spoke of God's judgment but also of God's redeeming actions. Ultimately, God willed restoration of the relationship between God and Israel. As we read in the prophetic literature, in due time, Israel was released from exile and brought back to its home in Jerusalem. God wanted Israel to be renewed and to live in obedience and faithfulness to its covenant relationship with God.

For many Christians God's mercy is embodied especially in Jesus Christ. Jesus is the loving one who desires to forgive us and put us in right relationship with God. Jesus' offer of mercy is sometimes set in opposition to God's justice. God the father is portrayed as a harsh judge and Jesus as merciful savior.

This tension and even opposition between justice and mercy play out again and again in certain Christian theological traditions. Often what is at stake in the tension between the two is God's will, specifically as it manifests in the order that God created, established, and seeks to uphold. If we understand sin as disobedience and insubordination—that is, not staying in our place in the ordering of the universe—then merciful forgiveness without justice might threaten further disruption. To let mercy overrule justice seems to undermine God's will and God's established order. Just as a patriarch has to uphold the family—all of it, with its traditions and honor—God is upholding the order of the universe. He is right to do this; it is just. And it is even necessary, if outright rebellion and chaos are to be avoided.

When so much emphasis is put on upholding the given order or when order itself is so privileged, only acts of mercy that contribute to keeping the order operative are allowed. A primary example of this logic attends interpretations of Jesus' death. It is commonplace to say that Jesus died for our sins and paid the debt we owed to God for sin. An obvious question that many have asked is: If God is all powerful, wise, just, and merciful, why could not God simply have forgiven our debt, and so our sins? The standard answer is that God demands justice. Our sin is an offense against the honor of God the father and God demands payment, exacts punishment, and seeks to have his honor respected. That response has been criticized, in turn, for portraying God as too punitive and vengeful.

Fundamentally, in the logic of this view, God's motivation is not so much to punish, as to uphold God's order. God's will is expressed in and through that order, which sin disrupts. Restoration and redemption must offer a remedy for the disruption caused by sin. The debt must be paid, not simply forgiven. Punishment is due; there can be no general amnesty. Justice, the righting of wrongs, demands it. The righteousness of God's will requires it. It is necessary to preserve order.

God's mercy functions in the service of God's will, to right the disruption to God's intent and God's plan. God's actions are not arbitrary or capricious. They are, however, directed not by our needs but by his needs and desires and the purposes and ends of the order he established. Just as in a patriarchal family where the father determines the needs of the family, so it is with God. Father knows best.

Prayer to God the Patriarch

God the patriarchal father is all powerful. Even though he is also wise and good, the emphasis remains on his absolute might. God's power is expressed through direction and control. Its aim is to accomplish God's purpose: that God's will, as manifest in creation and in history, be realized.

God has power over everything. He is the ruler of all. Any other power or dominion is derived from God. The only power and authority human beings have come from what God has delegated to them.

Because everything comes from the patriarchal power, all our attention and energies are directed toward God the father. God the father is in total control. We get what we need and want by asking him for these things. In this metaphor for God, the forms and purposes of prayer are similar to those expressed to God the monarch. Prayer is most often in the form of petition. We direct our requests, for ourselves and others, to God and ask him to fulfill them.

We also ask God for forgiveness. We tell God how we have wronged him, express remorse and penitence and beg for the forgiveness that only God is able to grant.

We praise God as well. We may even flatter God. When we do so we are letting God know that we understand that he has all the power, that he holds all the cards. We, therefore, tell God how great he is and then humbly present our needs and wants to him. Always, we end our prayer with a recognition that God the father's will and not our own is what rules and determines the outcome of our prayer. Only God is able to answer our prayers.

To the extent that we cannot comprehend such outcomes, we may question God. When a great tragedy befalls us, those we love or the world, we may even raise our fist at God and demand to know why. However, the affirmations that father knows best and that God's will be done ultimately put an end to such questioning as we submit our wills to God's.

We try to please God, just as we might want to please anyone in power, especially a powerful father upon whom we are dependent for everything in life. We defer to his authority because we know that our fate depends on his pleasure. It is better to stay in God's good graces than do anything to incur disfavor. Thus this desire to please God may well be motivated by fear, especially fear of displeasure and retribution.

The Strengths of This Metaphor

The promise of God the patriarch, indeed of any hierarchical system, is of security and a kind of certainty. God the father is in charge. He rules the household. This strength is similar to the power and might of the God the monarch. In the metaphor of God the father, however, more emphasis is given to God's will as being for our good. God is not only ruler, but also provider. He is powerful and good.

One way that God provides is through the order inherent in creation. Our place is clearly defined. We do not have to worry about where we belong in the universe or in society. Who we are in God's order and what we are supposed to do are clearly spelled out so we know what we are expected to do and how we are to behave.

The scriptures and teachings of the churches contain the rules by which we are to live. God's will is manifest through them. For example, the Ten Commandments are often cited as a distillation of God's rules for life. Creeds, confessions, and moral codes provide overviews of beliefs and ethical behavior. Laws and regulations govern how we behave. To the extent that we live by these teachings and directives, we are following God's will.

If order is a high priority for us, if it is what we need to ground us in life, then this metaphor has appeal. Such grounding seemed to be what this hierarchical view provided for the college professor who was advocating it. She could accept all sorts of other changes in her life and in the church, because the nature of God and God's universe was fixed.

She also believed that God was benevolent. God is good. God the patriarch wills to take care of us. This too is part of God's promise and much of what is attractive about this image of God. Not only does God's providence offer security but also the promise that whatever happens in life will be ultimately for the good, including our good. The belief that

God will make a way out of no way or will intervene in due time or will right wrongs whether in this life or in the next can offer comfort and support. When our immediate experience is that life is chaotic or out of control, believing that there is a given order and that God is in control of it and of us can make a significant difference in our ability to persevere, maintain faith, and have hope.

The Limitations of This Metaphor

The metaphor of God as a patriarchal father seems too narrow and limiting. It defines God's will as an instrument of God's power and that power is understood to be controlling and dominating. It is power over. In the logic of this metaphor, God's justice is reduced to judgment and God's love to mercy.

The right relationship we have with God is a formal one, of a subordinate to a superior, of a child to a formidable parent. God provides and we accept, gratefully and humbly. There is no room for reciprocity or mutuality or even closeness in such a relationship.

Functionally, a major limitation of this metaphor—as was the case with God as monarch—is that many people no longer live in the type of patriarchal world the metaphor assumes. Many religions, especially in their more conservative modes, may assert that God's world is hierarchical and patriarchal and even try to establish such social and political structures in the world, as well as in their religious communities. However, such hierarchical structures are antithetical to the practice of freedom and democracy that are central values of our society. In our world, a hierarchical model, ruled by an all powerful patriarch, is at best one type of social structure and one model of religious ordering among many.

That recognition of pluralism is itself antithetical to the logic of this model. Inherent to the hierarchical worldview, with God all powerful atop the hierarchy, is the assertion that it is the only reality, the absolute nature of things.

Patriarchal structures also lend themselves to abuses. The concentration of power at the top makes it difficult to hold those with power accountable. When power is understood as control over others, the danger of the powerful using their power against the less powerful is ever present. Husbands abuse wives, parents abuse children, clergy abuse laity, and humans abuse nature.

If God is the patriarch at the head of such structures then questions naturally arise about whether God supports abusive behavior and whether God's will is not used to harm people. If God is the ultimate authority, if all power is derived from God, if God's will is always good and right, then how do we account for the ways that people are abused and injured? The only way to answer such questions within this metaphor is to submit to God's will as right and good, whatever happens. But such submission may further intensify the harm of abuse.

This metaphor both reflects and produces a static universe. Change is seen as challenge and threat. Stability, with everything and everyone in its proper place, is highly valued. In an ever-changing world, God the patriarch can only be positioned over against the world, in judgment. God's will is to oppose most of the changes happening in the world and in society and to see them as dangerous and threatening. Such a perspective produces more and more disjunction between people's lived experiences and what they know of God's will.

Finally, this metaphor for God is problematic because the patriarchal God is necessarily male. Females can neither image God nor are they supposed to act like God by exercising will and power. Women are, by nature, subordinate to and dependent on men. At best, they are limited to their separate sphere, traditionally defined by motherhood and household duties.

This is the way God intended things to be. It is God's will. And father knows best.

4

THE PRODIGAL SON REVISITED

GOD THE MERCIFUL FATHER

THE STORY OF THE PRODIGAL SON is one of the best known and loved in the Bible. In the Gospel of Luke, Jesus tells it as a parable, a teaching tool: a man, wealthy with property and servants, had two sons. The younger son asks his father for his inheritance. Then he leaves home and spends it all in indulgent, wasteful living. After having squandered his inheritance, this son finds himself living in terrible poverty. Due to a famine, he is starving. When he remembers that his father's servants are better off than he is, he says to himself: "I will get up and go to my father, and I will say to him, 'Father, I have sinned against heaven and before you; I am no longer worthy to be called your son; treat me like one of your hired hands'" (Luke 15:18-19). So the son sets out to go home.

When the father, as the story reads, sees the son approaching in the distance, he is "filled with compassion." He is so glad for his son's return that he runs out to meet him. The son delivers the speech he has prepared for his father. The father, however, receives him not as a servant, but as an honored guest. He orders the household servants to adorn the son with fine robes and jewels and to prepare a feast to celebrate the son's return. The father declares: "Let us eat and celebrate; for this son of mine was dead and is alive again; he was lost and is found!" (Luke 15:23-24).

Meanwhile, when the elder son, the responsible one who had stayed home and done all that his father had asked, finds out what is happening, he becomes angry. He protests to his father that, for all his hard work and obedience, he has not been treated so well. The father never threw a party for him, he complains. In response to this jealousy, the father points out that all that he has belongs to this responsible elder son, but the profligate one who had been lost has now returned. This is indeed cause for rejoicing. And so the parable ends.

The prodigal son is a frequent subject in Christian preaching and a popular image in art. Whatever Jesus or the author of Luke may have intended by this parable, it has been interpreted as emblematic of God as a loving and merciful father. This God the father is like the father in the parable. He is a kinder, gentler patriarch than we encountered in the previous chapter. This is the God who, the Bible tells us, is slow to anger, merciful, and full of loving kindness. This God as father is ready to receive all who turn to him in repentance and awareness of their wrongdoing. Indeed, he goes out to meet them, even when they are still far off, and welcomes their return home.

God's Mercy Reigns Supreme

In this metaphor for God, the will of God, as loving father, is for mercy. God wants to forgive us and receive us back into his loving arms. No matter what we have done, or how far we have strayed, God will forgive us and restore us. He is ever ready to welcome our return. The supreme witness to such eagerness is the belief that God the father gave his own Son to die "for us."

Such mercy does not diminish or change God's power. This God of mercy is still totally in charge. He continues to be a patriarch whose will is supreme. The hierarchy, with God at the top, remains intact. However, in the tension between God's wrath and mercy, power and love, judgment and forgiveness, God tips the balance toward mercy, love, and forgiveness. The tension is not resolved; it persists. What is different is that God responds more from the side of mercy rather than wrath.

As the story of the prodigal son suggests, judgment is not dissolved in such mercy. When the father responds to the older son's complaint regarding justice, he tells that son that he will receive fully what is due him. The inheritance squandered by the younger son will not be replaced. This wayward son may be forgiven and his wrongdoing may even be forgotten, but mercy does not absolve accountability. Mercy focuses on repentance and a turning of one's will back toward the father's will. The wayward son's return is to the father and his will.

There are many references in the Hebrew scripture to God's mercy and God's compassion. The psalms are full of them, as are the writings of the prophets. For example, Psalm 51, a penitential psalm, calls on God to forgive the psalmist's sin:

> Have mercy on me, O God,
>   according to your steadfast love;
> according to your abundant mercy
>   blot out my transgressions. . . .
>
> For I know my transgression,
>   and my sin is ever before me.
> Against you, you alone, have I sinned,
>   and done what is evil in your sight,
> so that you are justified in your sentence
>   and blameless when you pass judgment. . . .
>
> Create in me a clean heart, O God,
>   and put a new and right spirit within me.
> Do not case me away from your presence,
>   and do not take your holy spirit from me.
> Restore to me the joy of your salvation,
>   and sustain in me a willing spirit.
>   (verses 1, 3-4, 10-12)

Again and again throughout the Hebrew scripture, God's anger rises up against Israel for all its transgressions, for all the ways in which the people have not kept the covenant laws and remained faithful. In those instances God decides to have mercy, to return Israel to the covenant and to right relationship. The emphasis is on God's power expressed as mercy. God could will anything. He would be in the right to punish Israel forever and even destroy Israel. Instead God wills to be merciful. God's mercy is a powerful expression of God's will.

Perhaps the most striking example of this dynamic is found in the prophetic book of Hosea, which likens Israel to an adulterous wife who has been unfaithful to the covenant. For much of the book, God expresses great anger and judgment, railing against Israel and describing a variety of punishments. By all rights God, as Israel's husband and covenant partner, would be justified and right to cut ties with Israel and sever the covenant. But then the God of Israel forbears: "How can I give you up, Ephraim? How can I hand you over, O Israel? . . . My heart recoils within me; my compassion grows warm and tender. I will not execute my fierce anger" (Hosea 11:8-9). In the end God restores Israel to relationship and covenant faithfulness: "I will heal their disloyalty; I will love them freely, for my anger has turned from them" (14:4).

In such biblical accounts God remains all powerful. In fact, his power is so great that he directs the events of history to fulfill his will. He even sends the people of Israel into exile as judgment and punishment and then returns them to Jerusalem. He renews the covenant and reminds Israel of his own fidelity: "I have loved you with an everlasting love; therefore I have continued my faithfulness to you. Again I will build you, and you shall be built" (Jeremiah 31:3-4).

This patriarchal God is still in control of all. He continues to know best, but that knowledge is directed more by mercy and love. God is also more patient and even more willing to wait for us to come to him. He is more inclined toward our personal well-being. This seems to be a chief appeal of this metaphor.

In our psychologically oriented society, with its concerns for self-actualization and personal development, the metaphor of God as a merciful and loving father seems more fitting than that of the distant, patriarchal father. A fatherly focus on children also makes sense in this child-centered culture. We are able to relate better to God the loving father. This is one reason the parable of the prodigal son, or as some prefer to call it, the merciful father, is so popular.

This image of God is especially powerful for those who need and seek mercy, those who, as the words of the prodigal son seem to suggest, are aware of their sin and are asking for forgiveness. The promise of this metaphor is that such sinners will be met not by the harsh judgment and punishment they may deserve, but by a merciful father. This is blessed assurance for those who feel lost or convicted of their wrongdoing, as well as those who believe themselves to be living contrary to God's will. It is balm for the souls of sinners who might well fear the wrath of God and God's judgment.

Amazing Grace

"Amazing grace, how sweet the sound, that saved a wretch like me! I once was lost, but now am found, was blind, but now I see." Those words from the familiar hymn, "Amazing Grace," were written by John Newton. They have spoken to people in all sorts of circumstances in the centuries since they were penned. Newton himself knew the power of God's grace in his life. An eighteenth-century, British slave trader and slave ship captain, he had a conversion experience, was ordained as a minister, and became an outspoken opponent of the slave trade.

God's mercy is indeed grace for those who experience their own wills as captive to sin, who are unable to direct those wills toward the good and their own well-being. God's will turns toward them in grace, comes out to meet them, and frees them from captivity. This willing mercy of God is a theme that runs through the great theologians of grace: St. Paul, St. Augustine, Martin Luther, and John Calvin.

St. Paul had his own experience of blindness before he was returned to sight by God's mercy. As the story is told in the book of Acts, Paul, the rabid killer of Christians, sees a vision of the risen Christ as he travels on horseback toward Damascus. Paul is thrown from his horse and left blind. His sight is later restored by the risen Christ, acting through the disciple Ananias. This ability to take and give sight is one expression of the power of God's will.

With his sight restored Paul is baptized and professes Christ as his Savior. Ever after Paul preached the mercy of God for one such as he, whose will, on its own, seemed obstinately contrary to God's ways. Paul became the great apostle of grace, whose witness was to the power of God to "accomplish abundantly far more than all we can ask or imagine" (Ephesians 3:20). God the father is the source of all power, which he deploys mercifully for our redemption and renewal of life. Through God's gracious will, we are made a new creation, able to live in faithful obedience.

St. Augustine, living several centuries after Paul, seemed to have had similar problems with obedience of will. He experienced his will, especially when it came to desire, which for Augustine included sexual desire and lust, as totally weak, incapable, and out of control. Only by God's grace, Augustine argued, was he able to do and be good in any way.

Augustine believed that due to sin, the human will had become so corrupted and so distorted that left to itself, it was no longer able to choose the good. Augustine refined these ideas in a historically well-known dispute with an opponent named Pelagius. Pelagius argued that God's grace was a necessary aid and companion to the human will, but that the human will was still able to recognize and desire the good. Augustine so opposed Pelagius's line of argument that he so much as said the will is captive. Human beings were not free to choose the good; they were free only to choose evil. On their own they could only live contrary to God's will. They would inevitably be disobedient children.

If Augustine's thinking is correct, then God's grace becomes utterly necessary to any possibility of goodness. Indeed, for Augustine, we only have life because of God's grace. Otherwise, we would be lost to sin. God wills not to destroy us, but to save us. God wills us life, and that is the sole reason we are alive, now and forever. We live by grace.

Centuries later, Martin Luther, the Augustinian monk, wrestled with his own demons. His problem, however, was different. Luther did not struggle so much with distorted desire and lack of control, as did Augustine but with his inability to fulfill the demands of what he expected of himself in order to be a good monk. In a way Luther's desire was for too much control. The more Luther tried to do all the right things and to fulfill the demands of religious laws and precepts, the more he experienced himself as falling short. He was exhausting himself and losing himself in the strictures he imagined were God's will. He felt condemned to sin and death.

Only when Luther let go and gave over control, only when God's grace came out to meet him, was he able to know that God's desire and will were for freedom and not control, mercy and not judgment. Such freedom and mercy were the experience of grace for Luther. They stood against his condemnation. Grace enabled him to fulfill the will of God the father but only once he let go of his own willful striving.

Luther's struggle was visceral. The liberating experience of God's grace transformed his life deeply. It became foundational to the Protestant Reformation and its principle of grace alone. John Calvin, Luther's fellow reformer, echoed the importance and sufficiency of grace alone, but for Calvin the centrality of grace was more about affirming God's power than responding to our experienced condition of sin. Calvin believed that our entire human existence is utterly dependent on God's grace. Without God's grace, we stand condemned. God's expression of mercy toward us in our sin is a sign of God's power. It is God's choice whether we live or die. The beauty and joy of Calvin's theology is that God's will is to have mercy, to restore us to life, though we, because of sin, deserve only death. According to Calvin and those who followed him, for that we can only glorify God and offer our gratitude and praise.

Dependency

In these theologies of grace, we are dependent—utterly dependent—on God. Without God we are nothing; we have nothing. The prodigal son returned to his father not because he could expect anything, but only in the hope that his father would not cast him out.

God the father, however merciful, still holds all the cards. He has all the power. For those who feel lost, this can be good news. The theologians of grace described above perceive it that way. So do those types of Christianity that emphasize repentance and the turning of our lives over to God. The fact that God is so powerful is a source of hope for those who feel helpless, condemned or weighed down by sin. Without the power of God—as a higher power, a fatherly power, a merciful power—we would be utterly and irredeemably lost.

This type of dependency is built into the philosophy of Alcoholics Anonymous and other twelve-step addiction programs. In these programs, included among the steps is recognition of one's powerlessness, especially in relation to the source of addiction. Admission of such powerlessness is followed by acknowledging dependency on a higher power. To be addicted is, by definition, to be out of control in some way. The role of a higher power or divinity is to be the other that is powerful and able to sustain control. The addict can then stop using his or her inadequate ability and turn over everything to that power and to the twelve-step program. Thus intrinsic to the dynamics of such programs is a view of power as hierarchical. At the core of such dynamics of power is a relationship of dependency.

For addicts and those who are convinced of their sinfulness, the realization that God wills to be merciful *is* amazing grace. In the mercy of God, they find rescue, freedom from addiction and/or sin, and hope for a changed life. God's mercy offers balm for the sin-sick soul. The trade-off or cost of such mercy is surrender and submission. God's grace may be offered freely, but it makes demands of us in return. It requires that we turn our own wills over to the will of the higher power, as did the prodigal son. His return to his father's household was to dependency and to obedience to his father's patriarchal will.

Compensatory Love

The appeal of God as a merciful and loving father is not only to those who are great sinners and addicts. It is also an attractive and powerful image for those who have not known love, especially parental love, in their own lives. Such persons find, in the story of the prodigal son, the loving father they never knew. If our fathers, and our mothers, were unloving or abusive, distant or absent, the affirmation that God's will is to love his children—all of his children—comes as good news. God's desire to be in loving relationship compensates us for what our own parents were not able to provide. God is the reliable, loving, ever-present parent. God is the parent upon whom we can depend.

This loving father is not only there and available, waiting for us to turn to him, he even searches for us. This loving God seeks us out, knows us and accepts us, just as the father in the story of prodigal son goes out to meet and embrace the returning son. As the psalmist declares in praise and thanksgiving:

> O Lord, you have searched me and known me.
> You know when I sit down and when I rise up;
> you discern my thoughts from far away.
>
> Where can I go from your spirit?
> Or where can I flee from your presence?
>
> If I ascend to heaven, you are there;
> if I make my bed in Sheol, you are there.
> If I take the winds of the morning
> and settle at the farthest limits of the sea,
> even there you hands shall lead me,
> and your right hand shall hold me fast.
> (Psalm 139: 1-2, 7, 8-10)

God is omnipresent and ever caring. No part of us is unknown to him. No aspect of us is beyond his reach. For those who feel lost and helpless, knowing that God can find them, however lost or hidden, can be a lifeline in their darkest moments.

For others, however, such sentiments may be unsettling and even threatening. In situations of violence and abuse, abusers often subjugate their victims by convincing them that there is no escape. The abusers will find them wherever they go. If the victims speak out, they will be punished, and if they try to resist, there will be dire consequences. Those who have experienced such intimidation might find the words of the psalmist to be more frightening than reassuring. For them the God portrayed in the psalm is not a loving presence but a predatory threat.

But it may also be the case that awareness of God's presence can counter the power of the predator. Knowing that God is with them allows those who are being victimized to feel that they are not alone. It assures the neglected and abused that there is someone who care for them and is more powerful than the predator. The psalms of petition and lament often call upon the power of God to overcome the power of those who plot evil and harm. Thus God's willing presence in all the circumstances of life may present a complex and even contradictory dynamic.

This image of God, as a loving and merciful father, offers more than constancy of presence and power. The merciful father is also generous in his forgiveness. In this way, too, the story of the prodigal son is very appealing, even more so than the God of the prophets. In the prophetic literature God has mercy and restores Israel, but only after anger, judgment, and punishment.

There is little judgment, however, in the actions of the prodigal's father. He does not berate his son for squandering the family's wealth. In that ancient world, in which the younger son's actions would have been an insult against the father's honor, there is no mention of the injury to the family or of the scandal this son's actions caused. Rather, the father's will is to be reunited with his wayward son, to offer mercy and rejoice. The return of the son and restoration of relationship appears to be more important than the family's financial resources or social standing.

Such an image of God and God's will may well be helpful for those whose own lives have been unloving. This portrait of a loving father balances the internalized judgment and condemnation that many people carry around with them. Young children who are neglected or harmed by their parents and caretakers tend to feel that they are unlovable. They pass judgment on themselves: There must something wrong with them if their parents do not love them or are mean to them. Children, whose parents told them they were difficult or bad, grow up believing such things about themselves. Those who have internalized such judgments and views might eagerly find the message of God's acceptance as healing and life-giving. If God loves them, if God seeks them out and welcomes them, then perhaps they are not so difficult or evil. Perhaps there is hope for them.

A similar dynamic is at work with those who grew up with a judging and demanding God, whose only experience of love is that it is conditional. Those who were taught that God is like the metaphors discussed in the previous two chapters may well experience the realization that God's will is for love and mercy as good news. If God's will is not only about power and dominance, judgment and obedience, then perhaps they do not stand condemned. They can rely on God to care for them and redeem them. This awareness is not unlike the experience of St. Paul, St. Augustine, and Martin Luther.

Given the contrast between this image of God and many people's experiences with their own parents or with what they have been taught about a punitive God, it is easy to understand how powerful and attractive this metaphor might be. The yearning for a loving and merciful father finds resonance in many of us. Even if our own fathers were good and kind, loving and present, would we want God to be any less?

The idea of God's will as desiring to forgive us, restore us, and welcome us home makes sense psychologically. The power of God's will, directed toward mercy and love, touches many of us in those places of our deepest needs. God as ever present and wanting to be in relationship with us is comforting, especially when we wander off course and find ourselves lost or under siege. The image of God coming out to meet us and welcome us home touches us deeply. God's grace is amazing indeed.

Our proper response is to offer prayers of praise and thanksgiving, as did the psalmist and as, we imagine, did the prodigal son. Even though he is silent in the story, how could he not thank and praise his father? How could we not thank and praise God?

The Lengths to which God Will Go for Us

Even though it is amazing that the prodigal son's father goes out to greet and welcome him, God the father goes even further to meet us and restore us. The merciful God, whose will is to forgive us and redeem us, gives his own Son, Jesus Christ, for our redemption.

"For God so loved the world that he gave his only Son, so that everyone who believes in him may not perish but may have eternal life" (John 3:16). This well-known and oft-quoted verse is cited as testimony to the extravagant love and mercy of God, who does not spare his own son's life for the sake of our lives. Jesus' death, as sacrifice and atonement, is the means of our redemption, the avenue to forgiveness.

This understanding of Jesus' death has enjoyed a long and far reaching influence in the history of Christian thought. It is at the heart of evangelical preaching that emphasizes that Jesus died for you and for me. Jesus died for our sins. Jesus died to restore us to the father. The great liturgies and prayers of the church rehearse the story: "All glory be to thee, Almighty God, our Heavenly Father, for that thou, of thy tender mercy, didst give thine own Son Jesus Christ to suffer death upon the cross for our redemption." Hymns extol the offering of Jesus: "What wondrous love is this, O my soul! . . . What wondrous love is this that caused the Lord of bliss to lay aside his crown for my soul, for my soul." Or "I come with joy to meet my Lord, forgiven, loved, and free, in awe and wonder to recall his life laid down for me."

The feelings expressed in these prayers and hymns point to a central dynamic of this metaphor for God and God's will. Jesus suffers for us, even dies for us, how could we not respond with love and devotion? God gives his only son for us, how could we not be moved? God offers us amazing grace, how could we not offer eternal and joyful gratitude in return?

The word *extravagant* is too weak a term to express the depth of God's love and the enormity of Jesus' sacrifice. Atonement theology, which interprets Jesus' death as a necessary act to save us from our sins, is rooted in this understanding of God's mercy and compassion. God goes to any length for us—for *us*. He does not leave us condemned, though condemnation is what we deserve. God effects our redemption and the promise of eternal life.

All that God Does for Us

God the merciful father not only receives us back into his loving arms, he also provides for us and does so lavishly. Just as the father in the story of the prodigal son ordered that a great feast be prepared, so God promises us such a feast. The image of the messianic, heavenly banquet as sign of our final dwelling place with God is the fullest expression of that feast. It is characterized by abundance, the overflowing grace of God. All whom God loves and saves are gathered together to celebrate and share in communion. Joy abounds in this banquet, God's pledge of all that awaits those who enter in his presence.

God's care, however, does even more. It provides for us throughout our lives. In the story of the prodigal son, when the older brother complains about the way his brother is being treated, the father responds to this brother's complaint by telling him that all that the father owns is his. God offers no less to us. He gives us all we need. He assures us that our inheritance is intact.

Psalm 23, another favorite, speaks of this unfailing care: "The Lord is my shepherd, I shall not want." God the father, or Jesus, is often imaged as the good shepherd who takes care of the sheep. A good shepherd does everything for "his" sheep. He leads them into pastures for feeding. He protects them and makes sure the sheep do not get lost. When any of them stray, the shepherd sets out to find the lost sheep. Without the shepherd the sheep wander off and are subject to attacks by predators. Just as a good shepherd rescues his sheep when they get in trouble, so God rescues and restores us.

Many find comfort in the image of God as a good shepherd. Psalm 23 is often recited by sick beds and at funerals. It promises both protection and abundant care for God's sheep. The proper relationship of sheep to shepherd, as of sons to fathers, is one of obedience. Sheep do best when they follow their shepherd and listen to his voice. Whether we are God the father's children or God the shepherd's sheep, we are expected to do God's bidding and heed his will.

Conforming Our Will to God's Own

The purpose of our prayer to God the merciful father is not only to thank God and praise him but also to conform our will to God's own. Such conformity begins in confession, in recognition of our unworthiness and sin. Just as the prodigal son prepared his statement of contrition, so ought we confess to God our unfaithfulness, disobedience, wantonness, and all other sins.

We come to God the father and throw ourselves on his mercy, so to speak. Knowing that God is merciful, we are able to confess with the assurance that this father will not condemn us, but receive us back into his loving embrace.

Our confession is accompanied by repentance or amendment of life. The word *repentance* means "to turn around," to turn away from sin and toward God. We not only confess our sins and our unworthiness, but we seek to change our lives by turning them over to God.

In this metaphor for God, as in the previous ones, all our prayers, whether of repentance or petition, end with the words: "your will be done." We give ourselves—and our wills—over to God. We submit our wills to his will. Father still knows best. Our obedience seems a fit offering and response for the love and grace that he gives to us. We show our love for God through our obedience.

We also offer God praise and thanksgiving for who he is and what he does for us. In our prayers we acknowledge the power and love of God that "saved a wretch like me." We also take note of God's mighty deeds in history, including the gift of Jesus Christ the redeemer. Given how extravagant God's love is for us, how great is God's power, and how merciful his will, our praise and thanksgiving ought to be lavish. Such recognition of God's care is expressed in a familiar hymn:

> All people that on earth do dwell,
> Sing to the Lord with cheerful voice.
> Him serve with mirth, His praise forth tell;
> Come ye before Him and rejoice.

Know that the Lord is God indeed;
Without our aid he did us make;
We are his folk, he doth us feed,
And for his sheep he doth us take. . . .

For why? the Lord our God is good,
His mercy is for ever sure;
His truth at all times firmly stood,
And shall from age to age endure.

The Strengths of This Metaphor

The primary strength of this metaphor is its emphasis on God's mercy and love. God's will is guided by mercy and compassion. As we have seen, this view of God's will is blessed assurance for those of us who are bent by guilt, weighed down with remorse, and lost in addiction or self-loathing. The good news is that God does not abandon us. As we hear in another well-known hymn, God provides balm "to make the wounded whole" and "to heal the sin-sick soul." God seeks us out and restores us no matter how far we have wandered, how lost we are, or how unworthy or unloved we feel.

God wills to forgive us. God's will is directed toward our good, but differently than it is in the metaphor of the patriarchal father who knows best. God the patriarch declares that whatever God metes out to us is for our own good, including punishment and chastisement. God the merciful father may also sometimes judge and punish, but he seems to care more about what is truly good for us, truly for our own good, and not just for the patriarchal order. So we experience God's will as merciful and loving, not just as demanding and full of judgment.

In that way God's goodness and love seem to win out over God's power. God could have destroyed Israel for it faithlessness. The prodigal son's father could have turned him away. Instead, the God of the prophets yearns for Israel's return and the father of the prodigal goes out to meet him. Compassion and mercy prevail.

God the merciful father seems sympathetic to our situation. He seems to be on our side. The power of God is used to help us. God is our advocate. He is approachable. We do not have to be afraid of him. His will is not arbitrary but rather responsive to our need.

We can have more of a relationship with this God. He is not distant, but comes down from his throne to meet us where we are. He gathers us into his embrace. His care is directed toward us. Especially for those whose view of God is as punitive or unavailable, God the merciful father offers a desirable alternative. This God is someone we want to be close to and love, not out of fear or duty but with gratitude and affection.

This metaphor for God also allows a more positive role for human freedom. God gives us freedom, just as the prodigal's father gave his son his inheritance and let him go. We may misuse our freedom and act irresponsibly, as did the prodigal son. Such behavior is not simply cause for condemnation, however. Mistakes we make and wrongs we commit may be part of a learning and maturing process. God wills us to grow and mature.

This understanding of God's will, as forgiving, merciful, loving, and even educating, fits better with our contemporary sensibilities. God the merciful father is more like the fathers who raised us or whom we wish had raised us. He is a family man who wants to keep his family together and in harmony. The togetherness of the family, the return of the prodigal son, is more important than the honor due the patriarch.

The Limitations of This Metaphor

A major limitation of this view of God's will is this desire for family togetherness. Something that has long struck me about the story of the prodigal son is that, in the end, nothing is different. There is no real change. The disruption caused by the younger son's leaving is set aright by his return. The patriarchal order, which was threatened by the younger son's request for his inheritance, is maintained.

The younger son does not seem any different. We do not even know how genuine his confession is. His plan to return, after all, began as a way to deal with his starvation. He figured that at least as a servant in his father's house, he would receive food and shelter.

The father welcomes his son back with a feast, which is both a celebration of return but also an assertion of the order that is restored by the return. Even the elder son's protest and the response to it, points to the real object of God's will: keeping the patriarchal order intact. The elder son will inherit what is his due. Things will proceed in the manner they should have done in the first place.

Imagine how different this story would have been if the prodigal son had responded to his father's offer of a feast by saying: "I too want to celebrate my having come to my senses and learned my lesson. But one of the things I learned during my time away is what it is like to be poor, to be a servant, to be of no account. I cannot let people wait on me. I cannot feast while others go hungry. Would it not be better to celebrate by giving some of our wealth to the poor? Nor can I wear these fine garments and jewels, when others are clothed in rags. Let us take sell these clothes and jewels and give the money to those in need." That's not the way the story is written, however. Even though the author of Luke expresses concern for the poor in other ways and in other stories, in this one, the focus seems to be on affirming the patriarchal order.

Again, how different would this story have been if there had been a mother and/or a sister who weighed in on the action? The total absence of women in the story is striking. Here is a family that seems to consist only of males: a patriarchal family through and through. What difference would it have made if a woman's voice had been included?

At the story stands, God's forgiving will is for restoration, not change. The goal of restoration is to set aright the order that has been disturbed. God may be gentler and kinder, but his will is still intent on preserving the hierarchical and patriarchal order. The merciful father makes clear that he is fully in charge; he holds all the cards. We may approach him in love and with less fear, but the power remains all his. He can choose whether or not to forgive and when. We can at best petition him and appeal to his mercy and love. His will rules and directs. The hand of this God, gloved to soften its touch, still directs all that happens.

Though we may extol this God as one who does not abandon us, we can easily feel betrayed by him. If mercy does not seem forthcoming, if we feel let down by God, the only recourse we have, within this image of God, is to continue to affirm God's will. No matter how loving God is, he maintains all the control and power. In the end all we can do is submit to the will of the father who continues to know best.

5

FRIENDLY PERSUASION
GOD THE NURTURING PARENT

WHEN I TEACH CLASSES ON THE NATURE OF GOD, I sometimes ask students to develop a job description for God and a list of the attributes or skills that God would need to fulfill that job description. The lists students come up with always emphasize God as loving and nurturing. They want a God who offers support, guidance, and direction. Most of the attributes they list for God characterize God as warm and caring. The God they imagine is like a loving parent or even a supportive friend. This God fulfills their needs, not as a magician, monarch, or patriarch but as someone devoted to their well-being.

Students also include on their lists, almost by rote, job responsibilities and attributes such as "creator of all" and "almighty" that gesture to the power of God. God's power, however, is directed toward the students' good and their needs. Rarely do students name God as judge. Even attributes such as awesomeness take on a different connotation. God is awesome because of God's infinite ability and because of all God does for them, not because God is to be feared or approached with wondrous awe.

In the last chapter we saw that even though the metaphor of God the merciful father seemed to move toward a more relational view of God, God still held all the cards and set all the rules. God's will continued to be directing and determining. God's intent was not only to have mercy and be compassionate, but also to uphold and maintain the order that God established, which remained patriarchal and hierarchical.

In this chapter we will encounter a different metaphor of God as a loving parent. This is a God who is intent on our growth and development and the good of the world. He, and perhaps we can even imagine this God as she, truly loves *us*. She is committed to the world she created. He is fully involved with history, not only in order to make his will manifest but to invite us into relationship and even partnership.

This God has an overall will for the world, but his way of operating is not simply to assert power or exert control nor to be solely in charge. God acts differently. She seeks to move us and affect our behavior through influence and persuasion rather than command. God woos us, so to speak.

We can still speak of God's will as expressed in history and in and through creation, but not in a way that is fully determined or determining. God wants to be in relationship with the world he created and, as in all healthy and vital relationships, there needs to be some reciprocity. There needs to be freedom, not compulsion.

If the relationship is to contain true reciprocity, then we need to be able to affect God, which implies that the nature of God includes change. God is open to influence—our influence. Our actions make a difference to God; they even help shape God's will. Such thoughts may seem new and startling given the views of God and God's will we have explored in the last three chapters, but in reality they are more in line with our lived experience.

This God is more like a parent in a contemporary family. Families today, especially in the modern and postmodern West, are child centered. Children have rights and voice. What they think and want matters. Parents in such families desire to be in loving relationship with their children. They make their children's needs, wants, and well-being their primary concern. Many of these parents have chosen to have children because they want to raise and nurture them. In such families children do not exist so much for the sake of the family, as the family exists for the sake of children.

This metaphor for God still imagines God in parental terms. God is the parent. We are children. God's job is to take care of us and make sure we are safe and secure, able to grow toward our intended ends. God continues to try to direct us and exert influence over us. However, God does not exercise control in a way that compromises our own freedom and agency. We do have say and some power in the relationship. We have influence too and can even get God to change his mind.

Biblical Sources

In one of the stories in the book of Genesis, Abraham enters into a "bargaining session" with God. God has observed all the sinful behavior in Sodom and is planning to destroy the entire city and all who inhabit it. But then Abraham asks, if there are fifty righteous men in that city, will you still destroy the city? God says, "If I find at Sodom fifty righteous in the city, I will forgive the whole place for their sake" (Genesis 18:26). Then Abraham asks, what if there are forty-five righteous men, and again God says he will spare the city. Then Abraham asks about forty, and then thirty, until he bargains God down to the presence of ten righteous men because of whom God will spare the city. In the end, however, the city is still destroyed for lack of even that number. Only Lot and his daughters are spared.

This conversation between God and Abraham is often cited as an instance of God changing his mind, in this case at the prompting and cajoling of Abraham. There are numerous other such instances in the books of the Bible in which God's will is not absolute. God's intent is not set in stone. God seems to change course in given circumstances. In the prophetic books, for example, God declares that he has heard the cries of the people or taken pity upon them, so he seeks to restore them from whatever judgment or punishment he has decreed.

If God is capable of such change, then God is open to influence. The sufferings, cries, and prayers of the people may have an impact. God is moved by their plight. God's compassion is aroused: "In overflowing wrath for a moment I hid my face from you, but with everlasting love I will have compassion on you, says the Lord, your Redeemer" (Isaiah 54:8). God who sent the people of Israel into exile, who punished them and deprived them, will now restore them. God's anger is replaced with God's loving kindness. The breech in the relationship between God and Israel is healed.

The Gospel narratives that attest to Jesus' divine sonship also contain numerous examples of Jesus' will being affected by those around him, especially in stories of healing. Perhaps the most dramatic example is found in Jesus' encounter with a Gentile woman, a story found in both the Gospels of Matthew and Mark. This woman, not an Israelite, approaches Jesus and asks him to heal her sick daughter. At first Jesus is dismissive of her. He tells her that he is concerned with the house of Israel and not foreigners, especially those, such as she, who are considered lesser. In fact, he refers to her in insulting tones as a dog. He says: "It is not fair to take the children's food and throw it to the dogs" (Matthew 15:26 and Mark 7:27). The woman, however, is not daunted. She remains resolute and persuasive on behalf of her daughter. She argues that even dogs are allowed to eat the crumbs under the table and so she challenges Jesus to pay attention to her daughter's need. Jesus seems to be moved by this encounter because he changes his mind and his behavior. He tells the woman that because of her faith the child will be healed.

In such stories of healing, the power of the encounter affects both the person seeking healing and Jesus himself. Another example is found in the story of the woman with the issue of blood. This story is common to the Gospels of Matthew, Mark, and Luke, albeit with variations. The woman, who had been bleeding for twelve years and whose condition had not been helped by any medical treatments, touches Jesus' clothes and is then healed. By the norms of the Jewish religion, her bleeding would have made her unclean. Not only did she, as a woman, break a taboo by touching a man in public, but she took an even greater risk by touching a man while she was in a condition of pollution.

As the Gospels of Mark and Luke recount the story, Jesus feels the touch and asks who touched him. Since Jesus is in the midst of a crowd of people, the disciples (in the Markan version) or Peter (in the Lukan version) do not know how to answer this question. They suggest that, since the crowd of people are all pushing and shoving, it seems everyone is touching him. But Jesus experiences the difference. This touch is not that of those in the crowd pressing upon him. He has sensed that power has gone out of him. In answer to his question, the woman confesses her act. Jesus then replies to her that her faith has made her well. She is cured.

In this story Jesus responds to the woman's initiative and behavior. In turn, she is healed by him, not because of what he does but through her own action. The healing is a result of her faith. In other healing stories, as well, readers are left with a sense that healing happens in and through the encounter with Jesus. It is not simply Jesus' doing. Rather, healing is realized when the sick person's faith and action connect with Jesus. The dynamism of the encounter releases energy for healing.

God Changes

In these scriptural examples, first Yahweh, the God of Israel, and then Jesus the Christ, God's Word, change their minds, take notice and engage in behavior that seems other than what they originally intended. These instances all take place in the context of some sort of an exchange, a relational encounter in which the change occurs. I will consider these characteristics of God—changing and relational—in turn.

For many, many people, it is a radical, if not blasphemous, thing to say that God changes his mind or that God is affected by "outside" influence. They also protest that Jesus Christ, as the incarnation of God, does not change. Is not God, after all, defined as changeless? Is that not what it means to assert that God is eternal and all powerful? God is the one who is beyond change, who is the eternal presence. "Immortal, invisible, God only wise. . . . we blossom and flourish, like leaves on the tree, then wither and perish; but nought changeth thee" is the way one familiar hymn declares the difference between God and us.

In Christian thought ideas about God and theological statements about the nature of God often represent a mixture or conflation of two very different worldviews: the Hebrew biblical tradition and the Greek philosophical tradition. The former uses metaphorical language to imagine God in personal terms: God exhibits emotions such as anger and compassion; God speaks and acts; God enters into relationship, in and through which God is known. The latter, drawing on Greek philosophical ideas, employs the much more abstract language of being and essence. God is being but not a personal being. God acts but not in and through relationship. God is not like us in our humanness but is totally other than us.

Although both the Hebrew biblical and Greek philosophical traditions emphasize the changelessness of God, they do so in different ways. For the Greeks change was considered a bad thing. They valued eternity and permanence and perfection as ideals. Change challenged the possibility of such ideals. In ancient Greek philosophy change was imagined as corruption, which in turn meant physical, not moral, corruption. Physical corruption referred to those processes of change by which a thing is transformed from one state into another. For example, iron eventually turns into rust and so is corrupted. The human body loses vitality: its skin sags, its organs deteriorate, and eventually a person dies. Death was considered the final corruption, so to speak. Processes of transformation meant that things were not perfect. Nothing was eternal or permanent.

Were these Greek ideals then impossibilities? The answer was yes, in the realm of this world, characterized as it was by change and corruption. But God was beyond this world and beyond such change. God was incorruptible. That is what was meant by perfection. If the ideals of eternity and permanence were to be preserved, if God were truly perfect, then God could not change. Otherwise God would be trapped, as are we all, in the corruptible and imperfect world. The words of the hymn, "Immortal, invisible, God only wise" portray this way of thinking. God, in order to be God, is apart from us, "in light inaccessible, hid from our eyes."

The Hebrews imagined change differently. For them, God's changelessness was not so much about the essence and being of God as it was about God's will. To affirm God as unchanging meant that God was steadfast and sure, that what God intended and willed remained constant. As long as Israel could understand what happened in its life as consistent with the stated will of God, then it did not have to wrestle with the idea of change in God. God's rule remained as unchangeable power; his will was clear and sure. But inevitably contradictions arose, as evidenced in the biblical examples cited above. What did it mean for God, who was just, to destroy righteous people, as reflected in Abraham's challenge to God? How could God, who had directed Israel to build the temple in Jerusalem, allow its destruction? What of the covenant promises that God made, in which he pledged to provide for the people of Israel? If Jesus preached the power and love of God, the coming reign of God, would he not want healing for all, even those considered foreign or lesser?

In those instances, the people of Israel and those who followed Jesus began to imagine God's will as changing to fit new and different circumstances. If the steadfast love and power of God, acting on behalf of the people, were to be true to the overall intent of God, then, in concrete instances, God might be portrayed as changing his mind. And Jesus the Christ might receive instruction from a foreign woman.

To concede that change occurs or even that it may be necessary is still not the same as seeing change as a good thing. Only in the modern era, in contrast with the ancient and medieval worlds, has it been possible to laud change and fully embrace a God who changes. Some modern theological movements even emphasize change as a good and necessary dimension of the being of God. They no longer view change as contrary to God's nature or as somehow a diminishment of God's character and God's power.

Chief among these is process theology, which draws upon the process philosophy of Alfred North Whitehead to suggest that being is becoming, in process, and that the universe is not static, but dynamic. God is not only open to and capable of change, but change is the essence of the being of God. Change is at the heart of God. In that way process theology seeks to challenge the biblical and philosophical traditions of Christianity and bring them together in new ways in order to celebrate change and to embrace becoming. It is no longer sufficient to argue that change may be consistent with God's eternal will. Rather God's will is for change; it is change itself. God in Godself is changing, and God is the author of change.

This fairly straightforward assertion fundamentally alters not only our view of God, but also of the universe. No longer is God's creation best characterized by stability. God's will is neither absolute nor unbending. It is not directed toward keeping things as they are, in a hierarchical order with everything having its proper place and role. Instead, God wills change. God's order is dynamic. Everything is in flux. And that is a good thing.

In this universe creation is in process, and so are we. All is growing and developing and becoming. God's will, no longer needing to maintain a set order, intends and supports such growth and development. The universe is not a finished product and neither is God. This way of seeing the world is dramatically different from more classical approaches. The clash between these worldviews, one affirming change and the other condemning it, continues to play out in many theological arguments today.

In and through Relationship

The worldview that sees change as a given and as a good thing often includes the notion that growth and development are nurtured in relationship. The relational web embraces the divine and all of creation, in a dynamic network of interaction. God is not to be viewed as atop this network, but as the grounding of it. Divine dynamism is present throughout the relational web. We will return to this concept in later chapters, especially as it decenters and depersonalizes God. In this chapter I will focus primarily on its effect on images of God as all commanding and as a patriarch.

In the midst of a changing universe, God's will is committed to being in relationship with us. God joins with us in the process of becoming. In that sense, God's overall will for the world does not change or waver. God wants the good of all, like a loving, nurturing parent wants her children to have full, healthy, and good lives. But the specific content and direction of God's will is not set. It changes as new occasions and concerns arise and as God is affected by the life of the world. God's will takes shape and draws purpose within and through relationship, in the changing circumstances of life.

God's relationship with us is not then based on control or simple obedience. God does not command or demand. Rather God operates through persuasion, friendly persuasion. God seeks to lure us to the good—our good and the good of the world. God acts through love. God power is expressed as love. God's love intends our growth and our goodness.

Ever in pursuit of us, God nonetheless leaves us free, both to refuse God and to respond with openness and receptivity. Though God remains the source of power and life and the author of creation—and thus we cannot yet talk about mutuality or full reciprocity—this God is open to our influence. In turn, God influences us. We allow ourselves to be shaped and formed by God. Such a relationship with God might be portrayed in a variety of ways, but most often God is imagined to be a nurturing parent.

God the Nurturing Parent

In the nineteenth and early twentieth centuries, liberal Protestant theologians put a great deal of emphasis on "the fatherhood of God and the brotherhood of man." God was father of all and Jesus, as God's son, was our brother and companion. He was there beside us, as an elder brother and a mentor. All of humanity was then united under the umbrella of God the father's universal care. We were all one big family, the family of "man."

No attention was given to the exclusive male imagery used or to the lack of a mother or sisters in the divine family. All of humanity, male and female, were meant to be brothers, reflecting the original and universal brother, Jesus. This lack of attention to gender, let alone to other differences, signaled a paternalism that has haunted liberal Protestant theology to this day. Enthusiasm for a universal family of "man," sharing one God as father, tended to obliterate differences and variety in deference to God's unifying, paternal power.

This father God may well want what is best for us. His power is directed toward our good. He is not concerned solely with maintaining his order or asserting his power and will. And yet, he is still a paternal presence in a male-centered, if not fully hierarchical, order.

The main shift accomplished by this metaphor for God is that God's love is now clearly in the forefront, and God's power is in the service of that love. There is no need or desire for God to demonstrate his power as evidence of his might or as proof of his place atop the hierarchy. Tension between God's power and love is resolved in favor of love. That love is manifest as more than mercy. God's desire is not only to restore us to the relationship marred by sin but also to nurture our growth within the family of all of God's creation. God truly wants our good.

This theme of love and a focus on our development are further emphasized in more contemporary forms of theology, including liberation theology and process theology. As we have seen, liberation theology, which attends to the concerns of the poor and the oppressed, tends to particularize God's love and care. God chooses sides, so to speak. He roots for the "underdog" and seeks to level the playing field. In that way, God is not impartial in his care. Liberation theologians refer to this phenomenon as God's "preferential option for the poor" and God's care for the powerless. What does it mean to suggest that God takes sides? How can that be fair?

One way to imagine this dynamic is to think about our own reactions, parental and protective, when one child is bullying another or lording it over a sibling. I, for one, tend to want to support the child being ordered around or treated poorly. In such a situation we may reprimand the bully or try to intervene in the situation so that all the children are accorded equal voice or are able to participate freely.

We may also work to empower the weaker child. We may encourage him to speak up for himself. We may let her know that we consider what is happening as unfair. Our goal is to support children in their growth. Out of love we direct our parental power to protecting and nurturing children in the particular ways they might need.

Much of liberation theology maintains a paternal view of God's parenting. God continues to be male and a father. The same can be said of process theology, though process theologians have been more open to viewing God in other ways. In recent years a number of feminist expressions of process theology have reimagined God in female terms, such as mother or Goddess. Some have even gone as far as to forego personal metaphors for God, focusing more on God as spirit, for example.

Given that traditionally women have more often cared for—rather than provided for—the family, it seems easier to image a nurturing God as a mother. This God's parenting style is child centered. Her focus is on the well-being of her children. She wants us to grow into maturity. This God acts through persuasion and leaves us free to respond creatively. A proper response to God does not mean that we come up with the right answer but that we use our God given capabilities and engage God in and through relationship.

Two other characteristics of God's relationship with us stand out; One is sympathy. The God of process theology is sympathetic—what affects us affects God. This means that God experiences emotion and acts accordingly. God's love is not characterized by disinterest, a distant regard. God is not aloof or impassive. Rather God regards us with care and concern. God's will is informed by feelings of sympathy, which give it texture and hue.

Sympathy suggests a capacity to feel for the pain of another, as well as to offer support and consolation. In the next chapter I explore more fully the implications of a metaphor of God as present with us in suffering and pain. In this chapter the emphasis is on sympathy as an aspect of God as a nurturing parent. A sympathetic parent is one who is ready and eager to listen. Such a parent does not does not judge so much as understand. She seeks to communicate understanding and concern. He truly wants what is best for us but does not presume necessarily to know what that is. She also rejoices in our joys and delights in our lives. He supports us in our bad times and stands by us no matter what.

Sympathetic love is compassionate in its understanding. In the biblical stories, compassion is a primary motive in God's response to the needs of the people. The prophetic literature contains many references to God's compassion or loving-kindness. God's compassion not only indicates that God is fully involved with Israel, but that God wants, truly desires, to respond to Israel in its needs and desires.

The other characteristic of God's relationship with us is freedom. God creates us with freedom and intends us to exercise our freedom. Such freedom entails not only the ability to choose but also to create. In the metaphors for God we have considered thus far, human freedom is more problem than possibility. The attention given to freedom focuses on the ways in which human beings misuse freedom to turn away from God and oppose God's will. Freedom is still affirmed as a good thing, but it seems to get us humans into trouble and to occasion sin. As a result, according to someone like Augustine, our freedom is compromised, so compromised that we cannot choose the good.

In process theology our freedom is celebrated as creative potential. Human beings are meant to be cocreators with God in the ongoing process of fashioning the universe and all that is in it. This universe is alive with energy and possibility. It is constantly becoming. We are fully engaged in that process through our capacity to act freely.

Such freedom is not independence, characterized by lack of connection. It is not a severing of ties. On the contrary, it is all about connection. Freedom is relational. Because we are free we are able to be fully in relationship. We are capable of more reciprocity, of choosing to love and be loved.

Freedom also enables us to risk. Our capacity for free action means that we are able to take risks for the sake of creation. Our relationship with God allows such risk taking. God welcomes and encourages our full and free involvement.

If such freedom is to be true, then the future must be open and not determined. God's will, and our wills, must also be open. Flux and even perhaps chaos are not bad things, but necessary dimensions of the process of creation. Imagine any creative act, whether it be painting a landscape or cooking for a dinner party. Some messiness is inevitable.

If all one's attention and energy are directed toward not making a mess, if someone cannot tolerate even a little chaos, then that person's capacity for creativity is diminished. Such a person will be bound by convention. They will always follow strict direction and paint within the lines, unable to experiment with a different color mix or a variation on the recipe. Freedom means that we can change the rules of art and the ingredients in the recipes before us. We can risk a wrong choice, for the sake of a potential breakthrough.

Parents who are devoted to the growth of their children know that allowing them freedom is essential to the process of their development. Children need to experiment and to test their capacities. They need to get up on their feet, take steps, and risk falling. Otherwise they will never walk. Children also need to be able to be messy in order to express creativity, as anyone who has ever used finger paints knows.

Additionally, parents recognize that such freedom is not independence. It is bounded freedom. Healthy parenting provides a safe environment for the exercise of appropriate risk taking. Therefore, parents put up gates so children's first steps do not take them spilling down a staircase. They do not let children play near an open flame or allow them to eat the paint.

Children are nurtured not only by their parents but also by the relational web that shapes their freedom and creativity and contributes to their growth. African Americans pay tribute to those who went before. They recognize those, as the oft-used phrase puts it, upon whose shoulders they stand. This acknowledgement underscores the fact that whatever freedom, accomplishments, and creativity African Americans might claim, these are not simply their own. They would not be who they are today without the efforts of prior generations, including those generations' sufferings, struggles, and accomplishments. This is true for all of us. Our lives are not private possessions or solitary achievements. Many generations went before us and many will come after. Freedom obligates us to never forget those connections.

A similar dynamic attends scientific discovery or discoveries of any kind. Albert Einstein did not come to his theories of relativity in isolation. Generations of scientists before him had already put in place pieces of a puzzle to which he added. Scientists around him, including his own wife, engaged him and offered their own insights and observations. If he had had no knowledge of those previous discoveries or if he had not had good colleagues, his own work would have been gravely diminished.

Creativity is a relational process. It is not an isolated endeavor, even if a person finds herself working alone.

The God of process theology is a connecting God, weaving bonds of sympathetic relation, as does any nurturing parent. God's will is directed toward our good, luring us into relationship, persuading us to join in the ongoing creative process, and calling us toward maturity.

God as Teacher and Coach

The metaphor of God as nurturing parent moves away from a God who is intent on directing our lives, but it is still a familial metaphor. God's will may be for our growth and development, yet we remain God's children. Another relational metaphor, which is less parental but still portrays God as helping us to develop and mature, is that of God as an educator or a coach. This God teaches us and guides us toward knowledge and maturity. She trains us and encourages us to do well.

If God is our teacher, then God's will fashions a learning environment for us. Learning environments include structure and step by step instructions or exercises to move students along in knowledge and skill. To be able to play a piano concerto, for example, students first need to learn about the notes on a piano. They need to practice scales and finger positions and movements. To play well they must develop some proficiency in the use of their hands and in reading and understanding music. A piano teacher creates building blocks of learning, establishes manageable levels of skill development, and guides students along until they have mastered what they need to know and do to play the concerto.

Along the way a teacher will correct them as well as guide them. She may also point out their faults and limitations and set reasonable goals for what they might accomplish. She will not, however, intervene in a way that shifts the focus off learning or takes the task away from a student, unless there is the potential for greater harm. If it becomes clear that a given student is incapable of learning to play the piano, a teacher may suggest that continuing lessons may not prove fruitful.

Additionally, a teacher may encourage students to take risks and be bold in their interpretations of the music. A good teacher is often able both to encourage and to correct, as is appropriate for each student. Such a teacher also gives due recognition to growth and accomplishment. He recognizes when students have reached proficiency and when it is time for them to graduate or move to the next level.

God as teacher or coach provides guidance toward growth and development. God provides the covenant laws to the people of Israel to teach them, as well as to direct their behavior. Jesus teaches in parables and instructs his followers. He is called Rabbi, which means teacher, and is understood to be the embodiment of Wisdom, that is, the divine acting in the world and providing guidance.

From God we learn the basic principles of life and are given the skills and resources necessary to accomplish the tasks before us and to grow into full maturity. As a coach, God encourages us and even cheers us on. However, God does not step in or intervene in the final outcome. This God is fully in charge—as a teacher or coach might be—of the learning and training environment but not of the whole process or its goals.

Whenever we undergo strenuous training or the learning of difficult skills, we may experience a certain measure of suffering along the way. Such suffering is for the sake of accomplishing the goal. It is part of the process of development. God neither causes the suffering nor takes it away. To the extent that it will help us accomplish our goal or accompanies the necessary risks we undertake, God does not intervene.

The medieval mystic, Julian of Norwich, wrote about suffering in this way. Just as a child cannot learn to walk without falling, God as mother, suggests Julian, may teach her children by allowing them to take risks and to fall, but never to the point that they are unduly harmed. In the end, declares Julian, "all will be well."

A Spirit of Cooperation

Both God as parent and God as teacher/coach will what seems best for us and for the world, with a deep and genuine commitment to the good of all. At the forefront of God's regard is genuine concern for human well-being and the world's flourishing.

This God also wants us to respond to her with openness, commitment, and joy. God's desire for relationship is met by our loving God back for loving us. God's ongoing creative activity is enhanced by our cooperation in creation. As we grow into the full stature of God's creative intent, we honor God and fulfill God's will.

Our will then is not opposed to God's unless we seek something less than the good, something other than growth. As long as we practice love and justice and embrace creativity and freedom, we are fulfilling God's will. When we do not, God seeks to persuade us and lure us, to bring us back into cooperation. God changes in the process as well, as she is affected by the life and needs of the world.

Prayer helps us along the way. We pray to God for guidance and for insight. We also give thanks to God for the blessings of life and for the gifts we have, including freedom and creativity. Because we know that we do not always choose the right or the good thing, we also pray for correction and redirection. Such confession is not pleading for forgiveness so much as recognizing failings or wrongs and expressing the desire to amend our lives.

Our prayer is also for the world so that God's will for the good may be manifest in the lives of all people and in the events of the world. God's persuading will and luring spirit seek to draw the whole world to him.

In prayer we are not simply petitioning a God who is powerful when we are not, but we are seeking to join our lives, wills, and spirits with God's, as expressed in the familiar hymn:

> Day by day, dear Lord, of thee three things I pray:
> to see thee more clearly,
> love thee more dearly,
> follow thee more nearly, day by day.

We may still say "your will be done," but not necessarily out of a spirit of obedience or submission. Our desire is for cooperation as well as comprehension and cohesion. Ultimately, we hope to unite our spirits with the one who is the source of all.

The Strengths of This Metaphor

With this metaphor for God, we have begun to shift direction. The universe is no longer necessarily hierarchical, a vertical grading of power and of value. We are moving horizontally. The playing field is more level, though not completely so. God is still the parent or the teacher, the grown-up who knows more and whose job it is to take care of us. In turn, our role is to be taken care of, trained, and taught.

However, this God's "school of souls" is neither a reformatory school nor a military academy with strict rules and a fixed chain of command. God is not interested in lording it over us. Nor is God committed to a given order that must be preserved at all cost. God's power is more diffused, even shared. It is most often deployed in the service of love and goodness. Human freedom plays more of a role not only in the life of the world but in relationship with God.

We no longer have to fear God. God understands us in a sympathetic way. While obedience is still a virtue, it is not directed to external authority. We are obedient and we conform our will to God's, because *we* know it is for our own good. God does not simply declare what is for our good, but God does seek to persuade us of it. God's will is something we embrace as a value and that we choose in freedom.

Two other values of this metaphor are relationship and process. At the heart of God the nurturing parent is relationship. God wants to be in relationship and enters so fully into relationship with us that God is willing to be persuaded by us and to change. God in relationship includes a type of vulnerability. This God is freely able to express desire and a range of emotions, including love and anger, as well as sympathy and understanding.

All is in process. God affirms that we are not finished products; neither is the universe and ultimately neither is God. The process is open-ended. Everything and everyone are becoming, in dynamic motion. This is a particularly important strength of this metaphor. Change can then be viewed as a good thing, not simply as loss or decay. Change is to be embraced, rather than feared.

We know from science that we do not live in a static universe. Nothing is fixed or unchanging in the created world. For too long, theological concepts that affirmed stability have been out of sync not only with science but also with people's lived experience. Process theology offers a way of thinking about God that is more congruent with our scientific knowledge of the universe and with the worldviews of modernity and postmodernity.

God as a nurturing parent may be either male or female, so this metaphor begins to break through the necessarily male and patriarchal imagery that has attended the metaphors for God considered in the previous chapters. There is even room for moving away from familial and paternal renderings of God by imagining God as teacher or coach or even as spirit. What is common to all these conceptions is a relational focus that is more centered on the world and its needs.

Lastly, this metaphor for God begins to redefine God's power. The emphasis here in neither on God's might nor the absoluteness of God's power. Power is for the purpose of life. It is in the service of love and goodness.

The Limitations of This Metaphor

God may be a fully benevolent father, but he is still head of the household. God's household may be child-centered, but power is not fully shared. Thus, while God the nurturing parent begins to shift away from a hierarchical universe with God, the all powerful one, at the top, this metaphor continues to be, to some extent, paternal and patriarchal.

Even when God is imaged as female, as a mother, the effect of such a move often reinforces traditional gender roles. The female God is nurturing and caring. She acts more out of love than power. Since, in a patriarchal social milieu, care and nurture are seen as women's work, such a female God does little to challenge social understandings of masculinity and femininity or of patriarchal fatherhood and motherhood.

As long as God is a parent or a teacher or a coach, our relationship with God continues to be based on need. Children are, by definition, dependent on the adults in charge. They may have freedom of will but only in a limited way. Students and those in training are also dependent; they need teachers and coaches. The adults, whether they are parents, guardians, teachers, or coaches, maintain more power. They make the rules and expect children to obey them. Parents, however attentive to children's desires and needs, ultimately decide what is best for their children and may discipline and even punish them. Teachers may work hard to educate their students, as may coaches to train their players, but, in the end, teachers give grades and coaches cut players from their teams. They set the goals toward which their students and players are to strive. Judgment remains with God.

Though there is much to be gained by softening God's will and viewing it as other than a force or given that must be obeyed, this metaphor does not sufficiently clarify the meaning and function of God's will. God may operate by persuasion and by befriending us, but God's will remains directing. We need to discern and obey God's will in order to grow, develop, and be good children as God intends. This view puts more responsibility on us but does not empower us sufficiently. For example, if the suffering that befalls us is a necessary part of the process of growth, then are we not to resist suffering or help someone else who is suffering? Or, is there suffering that helps us grow and suffering that does not? If so, how do we discern between them and who is responsible for the suffering that does not? While this metaphor does not see God as the cause of the evil that befalls us, it begs the question of what the cause of the evil is. If God wills the good for us, are we then responsible for our suffering?

Ultimately, this metaphor continues to imagine God's will as directing. At the same time, because God's power is not fully in charge, it leaves God's will too vague. In the interest of foregrounding God's love and goodness, God's power and ours are left to drift. God is expected to be a good parent, meeting the needs of his/her children. What happens then if God does not seem to be coming through? Does it mean God does not care or that God is not able? If God is leaving things up to us, what is the source of our power?

Power, unanchored and ill defined, causes problems for God and for the world. The final two metaphors for God that I will explore seek to bring power back into the mix more clearly. However, before we turn to them, we need to consider yet another version of the loving God's care for us—the God who suffers with us.

6

YOUR PAIN IS MY PAIN
GOD SUFFERS AND CONSOLES

In the introduction I described how often people turn to or question God in times of tragedy and suffering. When people seek out God in such moments, they tend to be looking for an answer to the question, "why?" Why did my daughter die? Why do I have cancer? Why was I raped? Why did my wife betray me? Why did God allow a tsunami in the Indian Ocean or a hurricane in the Mexican Gulf to kill so many people and destroy so many people's lives? How are these things God's will? For much of Christian history and in many strains of Christian thought, answers to such questions attributed the suffering to God's will. Those answers sought to find explanations and justifications for such tragedies, often in terms of God's greater purposes or God's judgment, perhaps even wrathful judgment.

Such explanations kept God outside of and beyond the suffering. Surely God cared and God might even intervene. Indeed, we wanted God to intervene. However, God was not affected directly by the suffering. God might cause the suffering, but God himself did not suffer. God could not suffer. Along with the idea that God remained in control, the belief that God did not suffer made it difficult for those who were swept away in hurricanes or diagnosed with cancer or whose young children were killed in accidents to turn to God with any expectation of empathy. They might look to God for explanations and intervention, and maybe even sympathy, but how could God know their pain? God was beyond such feeling, uninvolved emotionally. God's divine nature was sufficient unto itself. God did not need us, did not need to be in relationship with us. Such feelings and needs—and the idea that God suffered—were considered beneath God.

Throughout the centuries of Christian thought, however, there has existed another tradition, another way of understanding God's relationship to suffering. God does suffer. God may suffer in a variety of ways. First of all, God experiences suffering within Godself. In the Hebrew scripture there are numerous instances when God is portrayed as being in anguish over the unfaithfulness of the people of Israel or of suffering out of love for them. There is even imagery of God experiencing the travail of childbirth: "now I will cry out like a woman in labor, I will gasp and pant" (Isaiah 42:14). Especially in the prophetic literature, God feels deeply, including sorrow and betrayal.

God cares so much about human suffering that God also feels our pain. This God is not outside looking in but is present with us in suffering. God suffers alongside us and even in us. In that way God experiences human suffering. She does not remain separate or apart from human travail. God's love includes sharing in our suffering.

For Christians the supreme evidence of God's suffering love is found in Jesus' crucifixion. Jesus suffered agonizing pain and death on the cross. He also felt the pain of betrayal and abandonment. In all these ways, Jesus experienced human suffering. So we can relate our own suffering to his.

We might even feel that Christ is present in our suffering. Thus, for example, in *The Martyrdom of Perpetua and Felicitas*, when the early Christian martyr, Felicitas, is asked by her jailor how she is going to face her death by the beasts in the arena when she is crying out in so much agony during childbirth, she responds that then, in martyrdom, Christ will be present in her suffering, receiving the biting and clawing of the wild animals. In our own time, whether it be a rape victim left for dead or political activists tortured for their actions, the sense that Christ is with them and shares their pain and suffering affords them consolation and strength.

Not only does Jesus himself suffer and die on the cross, but the God whom Jesus called "Father" also experiences pain and suffering. Many years ago when a dear friend of mine who was a Christian lost his young son in a tragic and unnecessary death, I wrote him a poem of consolation in which I pointed out that God too had lost a son. Therefore, God could understand and share a father's pain. I was trying to tell my friend that he was not alone in his suffering, that his God knew what he was going through and had experienced it himself.

This affirmation that God is present with those who suffer, either through Jesus' suffering on the cross or God's empathy or God's own suffering with us, suggests a different way of being in relationship with God. The God who suffers and consoles relates to us as one with us. No longer is God totally other, even if fully loving. God's will is not simply directing or even guiding from a distance. Rather God is present with us, as companion and as one who suffers also. The promise God offers in the midst of our suffering is that we do not have to endure it alone. Nor is the pain we experience the last word.

This way of viewing God as the "fellow sufferer who understands," which is philosopher Alfred North Whitehead's ascription, has become increasingly more widespread in contemporary theologies, whether it be process theologies that draw directly on Whitehead's philosophy or liberation, political theologies and local theologies emerging from around the globe, especially among the power and dispossessed. The poor, liberation theologians remind us, are God's chosen ones, among whom God is most likely to be found. God enters into their suffering in solidarity and connection. God's presence and participation not only brings consolation, it also empowers.

A Tale of Two Gods

As discussed in the previous chapter, the Christian tradition contains two very different ways of understanding and talking about God: one rooted in scripture, the other in ancient Greek philosophy. Metaphors for the God of scripture are often anthropomorphic. God has feelings, gets angry, even cries out in pain. The God of philosophy is the opposite.

God is beyond any human images and feelings. God does not and cannot change. God is the source of movement, but God in Godself is Aristotle's "unmoved mover." God is not affected by anything. God has no feelings. God is beyond feeling. One of the main attributes then that the philosophers ascribed to this unchanging God is apathy.

We think of apathy as a negative judgment. When we say that someone is apathetic, we are implying that he does not care. We are implying that she is uninvolved. However, the word *apathy* comes from terms meaning "not" and "suffering." So to describe God as apathetic is not to say God is uncaring, but to suggest that God does not suffer. If God suffered and experienced pain, then God would undergo change and, as we have seen, such change was considered a bad thing in much of the ancient Greek philosophical tradition. The idea that God might suffer was scandalous to these philosophers. If God suffered, then God was not God.

This understanding of God as apathetic persisted throughout many centuries of Christian thought, although, as indicated above, there were always other images of God, often derived from biblical stories, that portrayed God as having feelings and being able to experience suffering. These portrayals coexisted with the apathetic God. Often these alternative images were found in more spiritual and liturgical writings, which by nature were less abstract in their ways of understanding God. For example, the medieval theologian and monk St. Anselm expressed both. He is the author of a very abstract theological argument for the existence of God in which he defines God as "that than which a greater cannot be conceived," and he also wrote a prayer with vivid and powerful imagery of Jesus as a mother hen wanting to gather her young chicks under her wings.

Beginning in modern times and especially in the nineteenth century, more and more theologians began to challenge the idea of God as apathetic. These theologians put forward the idea of God as empathetic. They advocated for divine empathy as a logical and necessary attribute for God. Rather than being scandalized by the notion that God could experience pain and suffer, they could only imagine a God who was fully involved, including in our pain and agony. The supreme evidence of this God was to be found in the person of Jesus Christ, especially in Jesus' suffering and death on the cross.

A Tale of Two Persons of God

Jesus Christ, whom Christians hail as Savior, died a horrible death, a criminal's death, on the cross. From its beginnings Christianity has struggled with this reality. How could God's chosen one be executed? Why did Jesus die? Why did God allow the crucifixion or, even worse, will it? Did God suffer and die on the cross?

Christians have also put the cross, Jesus' suffering and death, at the center of Christian faith. What does it mean to claim that salvation is by way of the cross? Or to believe that Jesus' death was for our redemption? Or to attest that in and through his suffering and death, Jesus conquered suffering and death for us?

Over the centuries Christianity has produced a variety of different answers to such questions. Many of those answers, in one way or another, sought to reconcile the seeming contradiction between Jesus Christ's suffering and death and the affirmation of his divinity and work of redemption. For many theologians, especially those in the early centuries of Christianity, who were schooled in Greek philosophy, the idea that God might suffer and die was blasphemous. Jesus Christ may have "died" on the cross, but God did not suffer. These theologians tried to craft explanations in terms of their understanding of the person of Christ, who suffered in his humanity, but not his divinity. Others challenged such arguments to the extent that they perpetuated splitting within the person of Christ. Were not the human and divine natures of Christ united? Was that not the point of incarnation? Ancient church leaders and theologians, in trying to find a way among such perspectives, affirmed the integrity and unity of the human and divine natures of Christ in principle, but were not able to find a fully adequate explanation for these dilemmas.

For other theologians the contradiction focused less on the person of Jesus Christ and more on God's will. Did God will Jesus' death? If not, does that mean that God is not all powerful, that evil forces had the final say in Jesus' death and God was not able to stop them? But if God did will Jesus' death, why did God make "his son" to suffer? Why did not the God who is powerful act in a way to spare Jesus?

Many of the answers to such questions propose that God may have willed that Jesus die, but it was for a purpose: Jesus died in order to save sinful humanity and to right a fallen world. Quoting John 3:16, "For God so loved the world that he gave his only Son, so that everyone who believes in him may not perish but may have eternal life," those who claim divine purpose for the crucifixion proclaim the saving power of Jesus' death. Unlike you and me, Jesus did not have to suffer and die. However, Jesus chose to do so in order that you and I might be saved. In that way, as this perspective argues, Jesus paid the price of our debt to God, bore the punishment for our sins, sacrificed himself in our stead, and took on the wrath of God in our place. The suffering he experienced was for the sake of fulfilling God's intentions for our salvation. Jesus Christ's suffering and death were in obedience to God's will, in order to fulfill God's redemptive will for us.

A Tale of Suffering: Is It One?

The logic of this perspective goes on to suggest that our proper response to God's actions in Jesus Christ is gratitude to God for saving us from the inevitable consequences of our sin, including death as the "wages of sin." Were it not for the grace of God, we would all be condemned to eternal suffering and death. We are totally dependent on God's grace, which we do not deserve and cannot command.

When Jesus' death is understood to be a payment, sacrifice, punishment, or substitution for our sin, then human suffering is often viewed as the result of sin. In other words, if human beings had not sinned, there would be no suffering. The same Greek philosophical tradition that made it difficult for early church theologians to imagine a God who suffers influenced those theologians' ideas about sin and suffering.

Those theologians believed that the life intended by God for creation in paradise, the life that Adam and Eve lived in the garden of Eden, contained no suffering nor, some argued, death. Suffering and death were the consequences of human disobedience. They were God's judgment and punishment for the "fall" of humanity into sin. It then follows logically that no suffering is undeserved, since all suffering is the result of sin.

Is that so? In what sense does a tsunami victim deserve death by drowning? How is it possible that a young child deserves to die because of a spooked horse throwing her? Does anyone deserve to die from hunger? What explanation is there for such seemingly innocent suffering? One response would suggest that in a fallen world there is no innocent suffering. Even though a person may be innocent in any given context, such as a young child who is diagnosed with leukemia or the victim of a tragic accident, the world, and therefore the context, is never innocent. Someone's sin is responsible. Traditionally, the only exceptions cited were cases of what is called "natural evil," acts of nature, such as tornadoes or viruses, that have no human agent. But even then God is exempted from responsibility for harm.

Such explanations may satisfy some, but they do not offer much consolation either for those who suffer or those who love them. They do not satisfy the thirst for justice and the need to right wrongs or the desire for comfort that we inevitably feel when we are confronted by starving populations or by the aftermath of natural disasters. We want more for the victims, and for ourselves.

Such dissatisfaction is a major motivating factor in changing views about suffering and God. Theologians, indeed many of us, want to find a way to talk about God's relationship to suffering that neither makes God the cause of it nor keeps God disengaged from it.

God Suffers with Us

The belief that God is able to suffer with us or is empathetic in our suffering is arguably one of the most significant changes in Christian theological thinking about God. The idea that God experiences pain, and with it the rejection of God as beyond suffering and apathetic (or *impassible*, to use the Latin term meaning "unable to undergo change"), is becoming not only more acceptable among Christians but more popular.

Some who embrace the idea of a suffering God do so because their views on the nature of God are changing. Others begin with the condition of suffering humanity and seek for a God who can help, who understands, consoles, and empowers. However they come to it, all those who argue for a God capable of suffering are opting for God's love over God's power. They are redefining the way in which God's power is understood. They are more willing to embrace limitation in God than to keep God distant and uninvolved.

"For God so loved the world" remains a slogan for such a view. Love is the essence of God. God's power is in the service of love. Therefore, God is willing to let go of the power of domination and control in order to enter more fully into a relationship of love and care with humanity—especially suffering humanity. God's will is still center stage and even determinative, but it is expressed differently, toward different ends. As the theologian Dietrich Bonhoeffer put it: "only a suffering God can help."

Some theologians draw on an ancient idea, the kenosis of God, to explain this loving action of God. *Kenosis* is a Greek word meaning "self-emptying." The kenosis of God refers to God's action of emptying self of power in order to more fully express love for the world. The scriptural verses most often cited for such an understanding of God are Philippians 2:5-8:

> Let the same mind be in you that was in Christ Jesus, who, though he was in the form of God, did not regard equality with God as something to be exploited, but emptied himself, taking the form of a slave, being born in the human likeness. And being found in human form, he humbled himself and became obedient to the point of death—even death on a cross.

In the nineteenth and twentieth centuries, a number of theologies turned to this idea to explain God's will, particularly as expressed through Jesus Christ. God's love is manifest through this act of self-surrender and sacrifice. The effects of such love are available for all those who are powerless and in need of God's care. Kenotic theology emphasized God's will as going to great lengths, even to the point of death, to make sure that God's creation is preserved and saved. As one hymn expresses it: "O love, how deep, how broad, how high . . . that God, the Son of God, should take our mortal form for mortals' sake."

However, it is not only Jesus who suffers on the cross and dies. God whom Jesus called "Father" is also involved in the suffering and death of

Jesus. But how? Does God actually die? If God were to die, would God be God? In the first centuries of the church, theologians who argued for unity of action among all the persons of the Trinity and therefore the first person of the Trinity's participation in the event of crucifixion, were accused of *patripassionism*—belief in the suffering of the father. *Patripassionism* was considered a heresy.

The notion that God could suffer, and perhaps even die, seemed impossible to those for whom even the idea of change in God was abhorrent. How could God possibly suffer? If God suffered and experienced death, then God was too weak, too human. Such a God could not be the author of creation and our salvation. The idea of suffering in God was rejected.

After all these centuries theologians still struggle with these problems. What is different today is that, for many theologians, the pendulum has swung in favor of God's suffering as evidence of God's love. If God is truly loving, if God is good, then God feels our pain and the suffering of the world. The biblical God, who hears the cries of his people and who is pained by their suffering, commands the stage, especially among those whose lives are mired in suffering and those who seek to respond theologically to such suffering. Like any loving parent, like any caring person, God feels empathy and compassion. The suffering of humanity affects God. God is the opposite of apathetic.

Jürgen Moltmann, author of *The Crucified God*, is one theologian who advocates a suffering God. For Moltmann Jesus' death, and God's presence in and to Jesus' death, is essential if Christianity is going to offer hope to those who suffer. It is Jesus' abandonment and Godforsakenness on the cross that makes his death an effective witness and action for the needs of the world. Moltmann argues that the death of Jesus is a Trinitarian action, fully manifesting God's will. On the cross, Jesus the Christ, the second person of the Trinity, suffers abandonment and death. The first person of the Trinity also suffers. The "Father" does not suffer death himself but suffers the death of the Son, as a parent would suffer the death of a child. And the Holy Spirit proceeds from the event of abandonment and death as self-giving love that maintains relation and brings life. The suffering of God is voluntary, which is to say that God does not have to suffer. God willingly suffers in solidarity with humankind, for the sake of our redemption. Out of love God experiences pain and suffering.

Moltmann seeks to give place to suffering in God by making the death of Jesus Christ on the cross a Trinitarian event. Others do not want to give suffering that kind of status. They do not want it to be viewed as an event within the Trinity or as part of the nature of God. To make suffering part of God, they argue, makes suffering good or necessary. They further argue: no one ought to suffer, nor should God suffer.

Whether anyone ought to suffer or not, it is an inevitable part of any human life. No one can go through life without experiencing some kind of pain, some kind of suffering. For too many people, especially the poor and those whose lives are shaped by injustice, suffering is an overwhelming part of their lives. Indeed, their lives are characterized by unrelenting suffering.

When suffering is the result of injustice and violence that causes injury and harm, then is it enough for God to suffer too? Is it sufficient for God to be present in our suffering, offering consolation and enabling survival? Should we, and God, not also protest against suffering and act to eliminate the injustice and violence that caused the suffering in the first place? Moltmann agrees with the need to act for justice, but it is the liberation theologians who have taken up that banner most concretely.

When liberation theologians talk about God's preferential option for the poor and for all who suffer, they are pointing out that God is not only present in consolation and solidarity with those who suffer but is empowering them to change the conditions of their oppression and to make justice. God's will is directed towards producing such change. God not only takes care of those in need, but also wants their lives to be better. In that sense God does not forego power for the sake of love. God mobilizes divine power on behalf of and with all those who suffer in order to eliminate the causes of suffering and to effect justice.

Indeed, there are different types of suffering: on the one hand, there is the suffering from the crushing effects of injustice such as poverty and lack of freedom; on the other hand, there is suffering that often accompanies those who work and fight on behalf of justice and freedom. So often resistance and opposition to the powers that be result in more repressive measures, including imprisonment and torture. Anyone fighting for good in this world will inevitably experience some kind of suffering for the sake of justice.

God remains in solidarity with all those who work for justice and freedom. God bears the burden of suffering along with them and does not abandon them. Many of those who have been imprisoned and tortured because of their political activity have spoken about God being with them in their worst and most painful moments, which has given them the power and will to survive.

God Is Compassion

The God who suffers and consoles may best be characterized by compassion. The word *compassion* itself means "to suffer with." The compassionate God suffers with suffering humanity and the suffering world. As we have seen, this God is not separate and detached but fully involved with the pain of the world. God's presence is in solidarity, never abandoning those who might feel Godforsaken. God does not stop at solidarity, however. God goes further, in and through Jesus Christ, to be one with humanity and the world in all their experiences. Jesus is then the compassion of God.

When we think about the character of compassion, we often imagine it as a quality of love. When we say that someone is compassionate, we usually are describing the way in which they express love and care. Compassionate love is gentle, supportive, and focused on the needs of the other. Attuned to hurt and pain, compassion seeks to alleviate suffering.

The capacity for true compassion is even able to see beyond the "presenting problem" into the depths of someone's pain, to find the root cause that may lead in a twisted and meandering way to the more obvious concern. Often it is a compassionate ear that hears, in a child's angry outbursts or sullen silence, mistrust of the world engendered by early experiences of abuse. Compassion can even guide the leaders of a society to embrace norms and laws that help those in need and set a goal of equal opportunity. It can also lead all of us to honor the differences among us and to be less judgmental of those in a variety of life circumstances.

True compassion is not simply a feeling or an emotion. Compassion is primarily an act of will. The God of compassion wills the good. God's will is for care and love. This loving, caring God even wills God's own suffering in solidarity and empathy.

The will of the God of compassion, however, is not absolute or guaranteed. Even though this God directs her will toward fulfillment, God does not seek to control the outcome. God does not ensure that all will go smoothly or well. In this way God's compassion is parent-like. Just as a mother wills the well-being of her children and wants nothing more than their happiness and the fulfillment of their desires yet leaves her children free to grow, so God does not control us or all that happens to us. Just as a father, however loving and caring, cannot protect his children from all harm, so God's loving care does not mean that no harm will come to us.

We remain vulnerable to harm caused by violence and evil actions in the world as well as by accident and tragic outcomes. There is no way to guarantee safety, let alone justice and right action in this world. There is no way to go through life without experiencing injury and hurt. The more we risk, the more of life we seek to experience, the more potential there is that we will encounter harm. And if we turn our energies to working for the good in places of evil, for justice in the face of injustice, and for freedom and right in the midst of oppression, no doubt we will experience the violence of those who are motivated by evil and greed. We will be exposed to those who practice control through violence.

The God of compassion does not come charging in on a white horse to save us in those circumstances. Nor does she abandon us. He is there, always, offering love and care and tender mercy. She weeps with us and feels our pain. He even tries to carry the burden of our pain himself. The God of compassion is ever faithful, even when we turn away from her out of anger or shame. Even when, for all our searching, we cannot discern his presence or when the mist of our ignorance or our spiritual blindness keeps him hidden from us, God is there, willing the good.

To the extent that we can perceive God's presence, we will feel comfort and consolation. We may also experience ourselves as empowered to continue to resist and to act. This is the God who even in death wills life. Such is the power of the resurrection effected by God.

Presence in Absence

Many Christian thinkers, especially in the modern and postmodern West, have come to this God of compassion because they see no other way to respond adequately to the evil and violence in the world and yet maintain faith in a living and loving God. In the face of overwhelmingly horrific historical realities, such as the Jewish Holocaust or the devastation of hunger and deadly disease among so many of the world's poor, no explanation that cites God's will seems tolerable.

To be sure, there are those who claim that the Holocaust or Hurricane Katrina were God's will or even evidence of God's wrath toward, in the case of the Holocaust, faithless Jews, and in the case of Katrina, a hedonistic culture in New Orleans. Those who offer such explanations assert God's power and control, even to the point of sacrificing God's goodness.

However, most of us shudder at such judgments. Even if Jews were unfaithful and the culture of New Orleans was debauched, the suggestion that the Holocaust and Hurricane Katrina are God's responses to such sin seems extreme. If that is the way God responds to sin, it feels disproportionate. We want to maintain God's goodness. We choose God's care over God's wrath.

Advocates of the God of compassion make a similar choice. They are also willing to forego God's power for the sake of God's goodness. Alternatively, they redefine God's power as an expression of love.

Some go further. They are even willing to risk God's presence to the point of absence. What does this mean? How can God be God and be absent?

In his Holocaust account, *Night*, Elie Wiesel tells the story of three males who are hung to death in the camp where he is interned, while the other inmates are forced to watch. One of the three is a young boy, who weighs so little that he does not expire immediately. Rather, he dangles from the noose to die a slow death. One of the witnesses to this terrible spectacle asks, "Where is God now?" As Wiesel recounts the moment, he tells the reader that a voice inside him responds: "Where is He? Here He is—He is hanging here on this gallows." Then Wiesel adds: "That night the soup tasted of corpses."

This story is often quoted by theologians who are wrestling with the question of God's relationship to the Holocaust as well as those dealing with other types of inflicted suffering. They interpret Wiesel's story as a morality play in which God is so present with those who suffer that God goes to the death with them. For these theologians this interpretation is evidence of God's love, persisting and manifesting itself in the worst of circumstances, even in the midst of violent and horrific death. God will die again and again, every time someone is killed unjustly and need-lessly. Jesus' sacrificial death on the cross is repeated in these moments.

These theologians' intent is to understand God as present even in seeming absence. Is that Wiesel's own intent? In Wiesel's story the inner voice's statement that God is on the gallows remains ambiguous. What if that voice were truly pronouncing the death of God, the absence of God? Is such death a supreme show of love or of powerlessness? In the story, those killed on the gallows had no choice. Nor were those forced to watch allowed to choose. Does God, too, forego choice in God's option for presence in suffering?

Christian theologians are reluctant to go that far. They may be will-ing to compromise God's power, to suggest that God's love is more effec-tive than God's power, but to relinquish choice would mean that God's will is ineffective. It would vacate God's will.

There is, however, a tradition, albeit a minor one, within Christianity that suggests that on Holy Saturday, God is absent. With Jesus' death on the cross, God is gone from the world. God is buried in the tomb along with the body of Jesus. The absence, however, as all familiar with the story know, is temporary. When Christ bursts from the tomb on the day of resurrection, the presence and power of God is fully restored. New life is proclaimed for all whom God chooses.

The image of God as absence, rather than presence, is a powerful one. If hell is defined as the absence of God, then we know we are in hell when all we experience is God's absence. The absence of God sig-nals danger. There is no good or powerful presence to which we might appeal. That feeling may be particularly devastating.

In Christianity such moments of devastation remain temporary: night is followed by day, crucifixion and burial by resurrection. God's care—and power—are always for life: our life and God's life. God hears our cries, even from hell. Compassion finally demands God's presence.

The God Who Hears Our Cries

The compassionate God who hears our pain evokes prayers of lament. The Hebrew psalms contain numerous such prayers: the psalmist pours out his soul to God; she pummels God with her complaints. How could God allow such terrible things to happen to him? How could she possibly withstand such defeat and persecution? Where is God when we most need her? How could God stand by and witness such agony?

The language of lament not only lists complaints, it rails against God. In the end, however, it turns into the language of hope, of affirmation. "But," utters the psalmist, I put my faith in God. I know God hears me. God is not far from my cries. God will take care of my enemies. I need not fear. For example, from Psalm 10:

> Why, O Lord, do you stand far off?
> Why do you hide yourself in times of trouble?
> In arrogance the wicked persecute the poor—
> let them be caught in the schemes they have devised. . . .
>
> Rise up, O Lord; O God, lift up your hand;
> do not forget the oppressed.
> Why do the wicked renounce God,
> and say in their hearts, "You will not call us to account?"
> But you do see! Indeed you note trouble and grief,
> that you may take it into your hands;
> the helpless commit themselves to you;
> you have been the helper of the orphan.

The faith of the psalmist is in the love of God that is able to hear and heed, as well as in the power of God to act. No cry is so weak or so angry that God cannot or will not respond.

Prayers of lament assume that anger and even railing against God are acceptable. We do not have to be afraid of offending God. We do not have to fear God's wrath. We can instead call on God to be with us. Suffering gives us that right, the privilege to speak to God without fear.

Lament is also an appropriate response to tragedy, to those occasions when nothing can be done to make things better and when little can be done to exact satisfaction. The nature of tragic loss is such that there may be no one to blame. We always look for the culprit, but even good people sometimes act in ways that produce much harm, without their knowledge or consent. Many of us are just beginning to learn the consequences for the environment of the ways in which we have been living for decades, if not centuries, on this planet. Now that we know, we are culpable. But think of all the harm we generated out of ignorance.

So we lament and we mourn. We grieve for all that has been lost. We pour out our anger and pain. We cry out in desolation. And in the end we entrust our grief and our unknowing, our pain and our confusion, unto our good and loving God. We do so in the confidence that God not only hears, but feels our grief. In these moments of lament and mourning, it is the God of compassion we seek. We look for comfort in her embrace.

The Strengths of This Metaphor

As indicated, imagining God as able to suffer is probably the most significant and far-reaching change in Christian views of God that has occurred in many centuries. Many people of faith have taken to this image enthusiastically. They have looked to God as compassionate companion in suffering to help them bear, survive, and even transform the pains and injustices of life. It is comforting to know that God hears the cries and knows the pain of those who are in travail. In the face of the tragic suffering and unrelenting pain, when arises the unanswerable question, "why?", pastors and friends may have no satisfactory explanation to offer, but they at least can point to the empathic and compassionate presence of God.

This God is companion to all who suffer, including those who suffer unimaginably. The suffering God of compassion walks into gas chambers with the Jews, lives with children on the streets of Rio, lies alongside the little girl each night she is molested by her father, is present with political prisoners in torture rooms, and weeps with parents who have just learned their child has leukemia. However much in pain they may be and however betrayed and abandoned they may feel, God does not abandon them. God is always with them and accompanies them so they need not suffer or die alone. The power of God does not take away the pain, but provides comfort and consolation. Their strength comes from knowing that they are not Godforsaken.

God's empowering presence goes even further, however. God also bears the pain herself. He takes on the suffering of the world, as a voluntary offering and sacrifice. By so doing God transforms human suffering and makes it redemptive.

Jesus' willingness to suffer and die on the cross was not only for, but with, the world. In this way the suffering God redefines the cross not as a necessary sacrifice for sin but as an act of solidarity. Jesus' suffering on the cross redeems suffering by God's participation in it. No suffering is, therefore, lost to God. No suffering is in vain.

God's presence in those moments, especially when people are being wronged or when they are suffering because of injustice, functions also as protest. If God is on the side of the poor and oppressed, if God hears and responds to their pain preferentially, then their condition ought to be deemed wrong, to be against God's will. The suffering ought not to be.

In that way, too, the presence of God in suffering does not breed acquiescence, but resistance and protest. It gives the oppressed the courage and validation to see beyond the suffering of the present to what might be different. It encourages a critical consciousness.

The suffering God begins to broaden Christian thinking about types of suffering and their causes. If God suffers, too, then suffering is not always deserved. It is not necessarily the result of sin or punishment for sin. God does not cause or will suffering, especially tragic suffering. Rather God takes on suffering in order to transform it and to support suffering humanity.

In that way divine participation in suffering functions as judgment on suffering. If suffering is not willed by God nor deserved, then maybe something more can be done to change the conditions that cause it. God exercises power for the sake of making right what is wrong.

This metaphor, more than any we have considered so far, redefines God's power. The character of God's power is known through God's love and care. Love and power are not opposed; they work in concert. As with the metaphor of God as nurturing parent, the power of the God of compassion is in the service of love and goodness. However, this God goes further. The suffering God is willing to relinquish directing power for the sake of love, for the sake of compassion. Although it offers no answer to why we suffer, God the compassionate companion in our suffering helps us to endure, survive, and even transform the pains and injustices of life.

God as loving compassion also allows us to image God in other than parental and gendered ways. Some may continue to find comfort in imagining God as a consoling and caring mother or father. Others, especially those whose suffering has been at the hands of a parent, may experience the opposite. For them, metaphors for God that are not parental may afford more comfort. Because Jesus is a primary symbol of the compassion of God, it may be fitting to imagine God as brother or friend or companion. We may even move beyond any such personal images to that of a spirit of comfort. These alternatives are more consonant with God's relinquishment of directing and controlling power.

The Limitations of This Metaphor

No one of us can get through life without experiencing some suffering. Further, the character of life for too many of the world's people is little more than pain and deprivation and violence. Given those realities the value of a God who suffers with us seems clear. But that value may also serve as a limitation. This metaphor for God may tend to give suffering more than its due.

In response to Dietrich Bonhoeffer's "only a suffering God can help," the question should be asked: "Can a suffering God help?" Or perhaps the question might be: "How does a suffering God help?" To a certain extent, when the emphasis is on God suffering with us, God becomes as power-less and ineffective as we are. God takes the evil of the world onto herself. He displays the value of sacrificial love. But then what? In the extreme, God dies. The world and all who are in it are left seemingly defenseless.

Further, when God embraces suffering as the crucified God and when suffering is the means to redemption, then suffering itself becomes a good and a value in ways that could be problematic. This is a charac-teristically Christian concern. It is an outcome of putting the cross at the center of the affirmation of faith.

To put it baldly: If suffering is good enough for God's son, why should we not all suffer? Indeed, many approaches to the spiritual life teach that the way to get close to God is through suffering. Such practices lend themselves too easily to distortions. There is a fine line between asceti-cism as discipline and as abuse. A key factor in defining that line is the way suffering is understood and whether it is given value in and of itself. When suffering is seen as characteristic of God, then there is a tendency to deem it valuable, as a good thing.

Even though the compassion of God implies judgment on suffering and even though God's presence may well encourage resistance to suffer-ing and transformation of the conditions that cause suffering, questions remain. Is the compassion of God empowering enough? Does God's power, expressed primarily through suffering love, tend to compromise God's power to enable life? God's compassionate care may offer neces-sary consolation in the face of tragedy, that is, in those instances when nothing can change the conditions of suffering, but does it provide the motivation and ability to discern when and how those circumstances are changeable?

Reinhold Niebuhr's prayer, adopted by Alcoholics Anonymous and known as the Serenity Prayer, comes to mind: "God grant me the seren-ity to accept the things I cannot change, courage to change the things I can, and wisdom to know the difference." How do we know the dif-ference? How does the God who suffers with us help us toward such wisdom? In other words, there is a tendency among those who embrace this metaphor not to differentiate sufficiently among different types of suffering and the conditions that produce them.

The wager of this metaphor is that ultimately goodness will overcome evil. In that way it continues the dualism between goodness and evil with God clearly on the side of goodness. The tension between God's power and love is resolved by subordinating power to love. Such an approach does not offer enough resources for dealing with evil itself.

Nor does it sufficiently clarify the relationship of God's will to suffering. This metaphor for God suggests that God does not will suffering directly, though suffering may be the result of God's action in the world. Even then God's care extends to compassionate presence in the suffering. For example, God does not will the crucifixion of Jesus, but God's incarnational presence in Jesus evokes the wrath of the world in a way that results in Jesus' torture and death. Jesus' sacrifice then becomes the fullest expression of God's compassion. Given this logic, in what sense is the suffering not the will of God? Suffering is not always the defining human experience. Thankfully, it is not the only condition of life. Is a metaphor that emphasizes God's solidarity in suffering adequate for the range of life's journey? What is God's will beyond compassion? If God's power is in the service of love and goodness, then is not God's will defined or confined by goodness but still deemed as ultimately determinative?

All Will Be Well

In the end, as the medieval mystic, Julian of Norwich, declared, "All will be well, all will be well, all manner of thing will be well." The God of suffering love is for us and with us and even in us to console, comfort, and transform. This metaphor offers the assurance that good will win out—God's will shall prevail. And in the meantime, we are not abandoned or left bereft. God is with us. That is blessed assurance for all who suffer. It is balm for the weary soul. However, for those who want more, including a more robust relationship with God, the help of the suffering God is not enough. They seek partnership with God and mutuality rather than comfort and relief.

7

POWER WITH US

GOD IN RELATION

BEING AN ADULT MEANS TAKING RESPONSIBILITY for one's self and one's life. Adults stand on their own two feet, so to speak. Loving parents want their children to grow up well and become adults. As the children develop, such parents give them more and more responsibility. Good parents try not to control their children's lives too much. They allow their children appropriate autonomy. Such parents recognize and encourage their children's growing maturity and adapt the ways they relate to them appropriately. They seek to maintain relationships that are loving and supportive, but not directing or controlling, with their adult children. In this process what changes is not the strength of the relationship but its character.

Because we human beings are born, and remain, fundamentally relational creatures, we always need relationships in our lives. We cannot and ought not go it alone. Babies do not thrive and develop without relationships. Contact and touch with other living things are as important for growth and health as food. When we try to go it alone, we come up against our limitations and our loneliness. We need one another for life, for living well and living whole.

This need for relationship with one another and with the world remains constant. However, as adults, our relationships are defined less by dependence and subordination and more by interdependence and mutuality. We seek partnerships of many kinds: with spouses, friends, coworkers, communities, organizations and even creation itself. These relationships make our lives richer, more enjoyable, and more meaningful.

Life together requires that we be accountable to one another, individually, communally and socially, and to the earth. We are not responsible by ourselves but in relation to one another. What we do affects not only ourselves but also those around us. Indeed, our actions may have an impact on everyone and everything throughout the world. And what others do affects us. The best relationships are partnerships of responsible and loving action for the good of the whole. They are characterized by mutuality and based on equality.

For adults seeking to be in mutual relationships and responsible partnerships, the idea that God is in charge and that God's will is determinative seems less and less fitting. If all is in God's hands, then in what sense are we responsible adults in the world?

The twentieth-century theologian Dietrich Bonhoeffer wrestled with such problems. He wrote about the world "coming of age" in modernity, which meant that human beings had entered into adulthood. The God who takes care of his creation as a parent and meets the needs of children who cannot do things for themselves no longer seemed appropriate in this world come of age. Bonhoeffer suggested that we needed to find new ways to imagine God's relationship with the world. The "God of the gaps," as he referred to it, who filled in the holes in our knowledge, who provided explanations for what could not be explained and who took up the slack in our responsibility for the world, was destined to become obsolete, especially as human knowledge expanded and science provided more of the answers for what had once been perceived as "God's will." Hurricanes and tornadoes, even drought and plague, could now be explained and predicted by those who studied weather systems, atmospheric conditions, and the spread of viruses. These destructive forces were no longer simply expressions of God's will or the application of God's judgment or punishment.

Bonhoeffer was suggesting that God needed a new job description, so to speak. Just as parents' roles change as their children grow up—just as they move on from changing diapers, to driving car pools, to dropping children off at college, to helping them move into their own homes, to baby sitting their children's children—God's roles in the life of the world needed redefinition. And just as parents who are unwilling to change and who continue to treat their adult children as if they are incapable of leading their own lives run the risk of alienating those children and even losing a relationship with them, so did Christianity risk irrelevance. Unless Christianity rethought its image of God and the ways in which God relates to the world, it was in danger of alienating the modern world.

Bonhoeffer may have been more sanguine about the world's maturity than was warranted, especially given the fact that he wrote during World War II and was himself the victim of the Nazi regime. Given all the irresponsible and harmful actions of human beings, against one another and against the earth, in the decades since then, there is much reason to suspect the capacity of human beings to be responsible adults. Yet this argument that human beings are responsible for what happens in life and in history continues to make sense in our world. Perhaps it makes even more sense precisely because of the harm we human beings are capable of. Ought not we take responsibility for our actions? While we may not be very careful or caring adults and we may misuse our freedom, should we not be expected to live with the consequences of our actions, as adults must?

Another possible limitation to note in Bonhoeffer's perspective is how much it seems to privilege the role of human beings. In a move characteristic of modernity, Bonhoeffer put humans at the center of the world. He may have asserted that the world had come of age, but it was the human person who was front and center, in charge of that world. Such thinking comes too close to replacing God with the human person, God's will with human will. It does not sufficiently account for the interdependence of all, including human beings with creation.

Enter the Web

God in relation, the metaphor for God we are exploring in this chapter, does better. It does not privilege the human person and human will so much as it emphasizes relationship. It does not focus on autonomous agency so much as interdependence and relationality. What is key to understanding God is being in relation. What is most true of God and God's will is relationship.

Such relationship is characterized by connection, partnership, mutuality, and dynamic energy. It is not simply that God is in relationship with us, whether as individuals, communities or even the world, but that the very nature of the divine is relationality. God *is* relational. All in the universe is in relationship, including God. The reality of God is as presence and power in and through relationship. We encounter the divine and learn about God in relation.

The Internet introduced into the world's consciousness the image of the web, the World Wide Web. When we think of the Internet, we might imagine innumerable strands of connection, invisibly active in multiple directions and across the globe. Search engines allow us to race along those strands to find and gather data. E-mail makes it possible for us to communicate instantly with many people in many places at once. Because of the Web, we are able to be connected, with people, events and information, in ways that were scarcely imagined a generation or two ago.

I still remember the party line, rotary telephone of my childhood as well as life before e-mail when I waited weeks for a response to a letter to someone in another part of the world. The connections were there then, but they were different. Now I can "chat" with multiple people from different time zones all around the world. Any of us can communicate and work and relate throughout the Web, instantly, simultaneously, multiply.

In the last several decades of the twentieth century, even before the World Wide Web established itself in the consciousness of many of us, the web emerged as an important and central image among feminist theologians and those exploring women's spirituality. The web imaged a central truth emerging from feminist thinking: that relationality and interconnection are at the heart of reality. Everything is in relation to everything else. Such relationships do not exist in a hierarchy, characterized by dominance and subordination along a ladder of gradations, but they operate on the same plane or perhaps multiple planes, in horizontal or multidirectional patterns that allow for complex, intersecting connections. Dynamic and mutual interaction characterize these webs of relation.

More than twenty years ago, when I was working as a university chaplain, I invited women in the university to join me in exploring women's spirituality. Since women's religious experiences had been formed in religions whose images of the divine and whose religious practices were defined by patriarchal and male-centered expressions, I felt that women needed a setting to explore their spirituality, on their own, as free from those male-generated and androcentric expressions as they chose to be. Given that most religions historically excluded women from leadership and from the full exercise of power, I wondered what would happen if women were the creators and agents and not only the recipients of rituals and religious practices. The women who accepted my invitation and I gathered as a group each week. We looked for ways to tap into our own experiences and find our own expressions. We sat in a circle and shared what was meaningful to us, equally and without judgment.

Almost from the beginning, this image of the web, drawn from women's literature and from attempts to find new metaphors for relationship, arose repeatedly among us. After a few months of meeting together, when we looked for a name for our group, "Web" was the one we chose and continued to use. I referred to members of "Web" as "Webbers." That term seemed to communicate the active nature of our spiritual explorations. We were creating the web. The women who gathered were ourselves the Web. The Web existed, and exists still, in and through our connections.

The image of a web is suggestive of those characteristics of the divine that feminist spirituality and theology emphasize. It connotes interconnection and creation. It is more circular and multidirectional than vertical or simply linear. The divine is not above or beyond but in and through the web itself. The heart of the web is relation, as is the heart of the divine.

The web is a significant and expressive image for the metaphors for God explored in this chapter, as well as in the next one. In the metaphor for God and God's will under consideration in this chapter, the web's deepest truth is that of relationship, that everything is in relationship with everything else. In the next chapter the more critical truth is that all, including the divine, is dynamic energy in relation. In both cases, the image of the web evokes and suggests several important dimensions of the divine as relational that will be discussed below: immanence, panentheism, mutuality, and shared power.

God in Here

For centuries church altars were up against the wall and the priests, facing the altar, turned their backs to the congregation. The message conveyed by this arrangement was clear: God's presence was outside the community gathered. No one was looking at one another. Everyone was facing in the same direction, toward God. The clergy said their prayers to the heavens beyond the sanctuary, where presumably God resided. God was transcendent, the transcendent one dwelling, as the familiar hymn states, "in light inaccessible, hid from our eyes." God was not among the people, not even in the church.

Then about forty years ago, Roman Catholic and Episcopal churches, in the midst of major movements of liturgical renewal, executed the simple, yet revolutionary, change of pulling the altar away from the wall and turning the direction of liturgical action. Now the clergy and liturgical leaders faced the people during the celebration of the Eucharist. God was no longer only out there, beyond where everyone was facing. God was presumably among the people, in that space created between altar and congregation.

In other churches similar changes were occurring. Preachers came down from pulpits built on high. They began to preach from simple lecterns or from the aisle, eye level with the congregation. New churches were built without raised pulpits. Some even arranged seating in the round.

Even though pews remained for the most part lined up in rows facing in one direction, the acts of turning the altar and changing the preacher's location reflected shifting theological thinking. Might God be imagined as present in the midst of the community gathered in worship, in and through relationships? Was God to be found through eye to eye contact rather than bowed heads or eyes lifted toward the heavens?

Meanwhile, feminist theologians were going beyond rearranging the furniture. They were chipping away at the splits that had for so long characterized Christian thinking: between soul and body, mind and matter, spiritual and material, sacred and profane, heaven and earth. The first term in these pairings, it had been argued for centuries, might be avenues to the divine, but not the second. Body, matter, the material, the profane, the earthly were not ways to God. Despite its doctrine of the incarnation, Christianity had trouble understanding God as having any connection with bodies and the earth. Matter was tainted by sin. Only the spirit might ascend to God.

In such thinking God has to be transcendent, totally other. This idea of God's absolute otherness is even more strongly reflected in Christian thinking about creation. A commonly held Christian belief is that God created *ex nihilo*, out of nothing. God did not need any matter, any material, in order to create and nothing existed prior to God's creation. This belief affirms God as fully transcendent and all powerful. God is powerful and sovereign enough to bring everything into being out of nothing. The presence of anything else, the preexistence of any matter, would diminish or defile God.

Given this belief in God's utter transcendence and otherness, imagine what a dramatic change it was to turn the clergy around or bring them down from pulpits so clergy and people faced one another at eye level. If God was in the midst of the congregation and no longer out there or up there, what difference would that make for how we relate to God? Or how we imagine God? Or think about the process of creation? How would we think differently about bodies and the earth?

Perhaps God was not utterly transcendent, defined by his total otherness. God could be found and was present in and through all of creation. God's presence might then be characterized not only by transcendence, but also by immanence. Or rather, the definitions of transcendence and immanence, so long determined by the splits between spirit and matter, mind and body, might need to be reworked. Perhaps they were not opposites or absolutely opposed. Perhaps transcendence and immanence were related and spirit and matter connected. Theologians, such as Sallie McFague, even imaged the earth or the universe as God's body. If the universe was God's body, then God was present in creation.

Panentheism

Panentheism, which literally means "all in God," connotes this idea that God is to be found in creation. God contains the world and is present in and to the world. The transcendence of God is not otherness, defined as total separation. Transcendence is not opposed to immanence. Indeed, it might be imagined through immanence, transcendence in immanence. This does not mean that the divine is equivalent to the world, an idea often referred to as pantheism, that "all is God." God is in, yet distinct from, creation. The divine is not exhausted by presence in creation, but neither does God shrink away from it.

If God is present in creation, then it follows that our knowledge of God and our relationship with God are in and through what God has created. We can find the divine and expressions of God's will all around us. We do not have to leave earth behind to find heaven. We do not have to deny our bodies to save our souls. We do not have to negate our humanity to seek God.

In a panentheistic universe trees reveal the stature of God. Mountains tell of the grandeur of God. Flowers, in all their variety and riot of colors, gesture to the transcendence of God. Rivers and oceans express the energy and power of God. Human beings reflect the glory of God. Divine mystery is as close as breath.

When we live our lives well, we are being God's people. In tending the earth and taking care with creation, we are honoring God. By loving one another, we are loving God. When we treat one another with respect and practice justice, we are doing God's work.

There is no hierarchy in God's body. St. Paul uses the image of the body of Christ to describe the Christian community. Each member of the body, each body part, has its function and role. All need one other to function fully. Even though St. Paul put Christ as the head, superior to the rest of the body, and so maintained a hierarchy, he still vividly portrayed the importance of each part's different and distinct contribution.

So it is also with the earth as God's body. Human beings are not at the top of the food chain in a material universe but are one among many species and creatures in an intricate and carefully balanced web of connection. Life on earth cannot exist without the earthworm's contribution to aeration. Nor would there be food for any creatures to eat without sun and rain. Humans would not have adequate air to breathe without trees and plants.

Each element is part of the whole. The whole exists only in and through the parts. The parts fit together because of the whole. All reveal God. God is present in all: from the earthworm to the rain, from the words of a poet to expressions of physical love. God is the matrix in which everything exists and has being.

Panentheism suggests that interconnection is an expression of divine presence. Everything exists in relation to everything else because all is contained in God. The divine is active in and through everything, weaving relations. God's will is for interrelationship. God created and infused all with divine presence.

The Relational God

Some theologians go further, or in a somewhat different direction, to suggest that relationality is the very nature of God. God in and of herself is relation or, as Carter Heyward puts it, "the power in relation." In other words, God is not just present in relation but is relation itself or the ground and source of our relating. So as Heyward suggests, when any of us are in relationship with others we are "godding." Our relationships reveal and express the divine. This approach privileges relationships and relationality as the essence of God.

The relationships in which we are truly "godding" are characterized by mutuality and reciprocity. The capacity for mutuality requires freedom: the freedom to fully become and be ourselves and to give ourselves to one another without compulsion or constraint. It also connotes equality. This means that in mutual relationships, there are no gradations of value or status or privilege or dependence that might order relationships in hierarchies. No one or no thing is deemed as better in any defining way.

Feminist theologians have pointed out that relationships of mutuality require and reveal the essence of God as love and the power of that love as "erotic power." Erotic power is the energy of connection. It makes love possible. It is the energy for life that brings creation into being. Erotic power is dynamic energy meeting dynamic energy for the sake of life. Nothing can exist without erotic power. This power does not force or dominate; it attracts and enlivens. It expresses love.

Erotic power is passionate, not dispassionate. Christian thinking about love has tended to privilege what the Greeks called *agape* or agapic love. Agapic love is extolled for being dispassionate: it acts not from desire, but from disinterested care. Such love is directed toward the other, to the point of sacrifice. It does not seek mutuality, but self-giving.

Many point to Jesus as the model of such self-giving and the embodiment of agapic love. The cross is the symbol of his loving sacrifice. Jesus gave his life as an offering and "ransom" for the redemption of the world. However, if we shift attention away from the cross to Jesus' life and ministry, especially his interactions with those in need, a different picture emerges, one that is more consonant with erotic power.

Jesus' power to heal and transform those who were diseased, possessed, outcast, and suffering operated relationally. The people who encountered Jesus experienced their lives changed in and through relationship. In the healing stories, for example, as recorded in the Gospels, Jesus often said "your faith has healed you" or "do not fear, but have faith." It is by such faith, which is the manifestation of erotic power or the power of relationship, moving between Jesus and those with whom he connects, that the "miracles" of healing and transformation happen. Indeed, Jesus can seem to do little when such faith is not present. When there is no real connection and so energy does not flow, Jesus' power is disabled. For example, when the people in Jesus' hometown question his authority, he is ineffective (Mark 6:1-5). Jesus' power is relational and without connections to carry it, nothing much can happen. The love Jesus expressed was the love of eros, dynamic desire for relation.

Reimagining Relation

These ideas—of a panentheistic God, or of Jesus' power and love as relational and erotic, or of God and creation in mutual relation in any way—

may well seem inconceivable and even dangerous to those schooled in traditional notions of God's transcendence and of God's will as absolute freedom. In the last two chapters we examined long held beliefs that God is not affected by anything and that God is detached and literally apathetic. We also saw how major streams of theological thought have maintained that God does not and cannot change.

Those who seek to preserve God's absolute otherness and utter separation also assert that God is noncontingent. Noncontingent means, literally, "not touching." Touch connotes connection and relation. Already in the metaphors for God discussed in the last chapters, we have come to know God as contingent, touched and changed by what happens to us and to creation. The metaphor of God as relational pushes God even further into contact, involvement, and contingency.

The idea of contingency also connotes a type of dependence. If my plans are contingent on my friend's, then what she decides to do influences my choices. My own decisions and actions depend on another's. Such dependence is not that of a lesser or weaker person; it is not dependency. Rather it is the dependence, the entanglement in the web or relation, of someone who enters into and commits to relationships that define and confine what we do, and when and how we do them.

When two people decide to live their lives together, they are choosing to make their decisions together in the future. They will no longer be separate individuals free to do what they want, when they want, with no strings attached. When they combine households and incomes and life plans, they are committing to living and planning life in concert. Each person's desires need to be taken into account. Neither person is in complete charge. Each person's will factors in. Often the troubles in such relationships are over the clash of wills and the differences in desires. These difficulties sometimes arise from the inability to be contingent, to work things out together.

It is not easy to be in such relationships of intimacy and contingency. Most of us work hard for them, however, because we feel more whole, happier, and indeed more human in relationship than not. We know our growth into the fullness of who we might be depends on our being in relation.

Our energy is multiplied as we learn the new math, that one plus one equals more than two or that ten ones are more than ten. Without relationships of love and friendship, unencumbered though we may be, we seem to wither and dry up. Whether it be in the intimacy of family or through friendships and community or the companionship of pets or by communion with nature, we are our best in relation.

Similarly, the energy and power of the relational God is manifest and strengthened through connection. This God is contingent. She is so involved with creation that we can say that God needs us, needs creation. What God does depends on creation. God does not act in isolation.

Again, such a notion of need in God would be considered blasphemous in some theological circles. The very definition of God's transcendence is that God is beyond any need. There can be no necessity in God. God does not need anyone or anything. As we saw, given the doctrine of creation *ex nihilo*, God does not require anything in order to create everything. Nor does God even need to create. Creation is an expression of God's power and freedom, not God's desire for relationship.

If God were to create out of need or desire, as this thinking goes, then God's freedom and sovereignty are compromised. If there is any need in God, then God is not utterly free, and if not utterly free, then God's transcendence and power are rendered contingent. Such is the logic of the traditional views that seek to preserve the sovereignty of God's being and God's will.

The logic of the relational God moves in a different direction. It goes even further than ideas about God's love we have already encountered thus far: that God empties himself to be one with us or that God is moved by what happens in creation. Those ideas bring God more into relationship, but God remains the other who chooses to love to the point of changing and even suffering for creation. The relational God, however, is *by nature* in relation. The divine is manifest in creation and in the connections that bind us. Without creation, without relation, God is not God.

Not only is God defined as relational, but the divine energy is what makes relationships possible. However, not all relationships are of God, and not all manifest divine power. The character of our relationships matter above all. Indeed they are the matter of God.

As indicated above relationships that reflect God's power are ones of mutuality. Mutuality means the relationship goes both ways. We not only seek God, but God seeks us. We need God, but God needs creation as well. The nature of the need—God's and ours—does not have to be and is not the same. Which is to say, we are not God, not the same as God.

Images of relationship that fit this idea of God are drawn from peer rather than parental or hierarchical relationships. For example, God is imaged as friend or lover or companion. Early Christian spirituality and the language of the mystics contained numerous such references. The first Christians were sometimes referred to as friends of God, a term the Quakers took centuries later to refer to themselves as the Society of Friends. Mystical writings are shot through with language about being in love with God and with expressions of erotic, passionate love. How else might the mystics have approximated the intimacy they experienced, the union for which they yearned? Others have turned to the language of companionship to express the constancy and sustaining presence of God. All these images are trying to imagine God *with* us. The power of this God is shared power.

Other images of the relational God are as partner and cocreator. The emphasis is of God with us, God's power to act and create is shared with us and expressed through us and all of creation. Some theologians turn to maternal images, not to return to a parental relationship, but to evoke the interrelationship of mother and fetus, mother and baby. The idea of God as womb, holding all of creation, is one such image. The presence of this God is through her body, the universe.

The relationships that reveal this God are characterized not only by mutuality but also by love and justice. The relational God seeks right relationship. We are in relationship with God, we are participating in God, we are "godding" when we are in right relationship. Right relationships are ones of love and justice. Abusive relationships that practice greed or bigotry or hatred, unequal power arrangements and oppressive systems, and the exploitation of others, including creation, are not of God. God is not to be found in such relations. Indeed, God opposes them and passes judgment on them. The power of God is directed toward equality rather than domination, transformation in the face of exploitation and oppression, and sharing and mutuality instead of greed and prejudice. The goal of right relation is wholeness and abundance of life.

God's Will in Relation

God wills goodness and life. The relational God is all goodness, which is to say, right relationship, love, and justice manifest the will of God. However, the will of the relational God is not controlling or determinative or even noncontingent. God's will is relational as well. It works in relation.

God's will might then be thought of more like God's desire or yearning or even passion. It is God's most passionate desire and yearning that all of creation live in harmony and abundant life. The relational God, by its very character, wants all to be well. But God's will, God's willing, does not necessarily make it so, neither now nor in the end.

Many who hold to this view of God as relational hope for the fulfillment of God's will in the end. Some even believe that fulfillment will be the case. Yet others realize that relationality and openness go together. If God is fully in relation, is truly the power in relation, then God's willing remains open and life itself is open ended. There is much of chance in life and in creation and much that is not the outcome of anyone's will, human or divine. No one or no thing is in charge in any determining way.

God's will then is not in control or set. What God wants to see happen, what God hopes for, remains constant in the sense that God's desire for life does not change. God wants goodness and right relationship and life abundant to be, always and everywhere. But whether, when, and how those things may come about or happen is not known, and cannot fully be known, even by God.

If God's will is open in this way and not determinative, then what we do and do not do matter tremendously. We are indeed living in the world come of age, with us as adult actors, agents of what happens. The relational God does not intervene from on high to save us or to condemn us. Nor does God act like the loving parent of little children to protect us or rescue us. As adults, we are responsible for, even as we are participants in, God's body.

We do not, however, bear this responsibility by ourselves. The promise of God is to be with us always. The relational God is in this life with us. And we are in it with God. God's power as dynamic energy is present with us, ever available to us. Indeed, it lives within us and within all of creation. God's heartbeat is that of the web of life.

Relating to the God of Relation

When we begin to embrace this metaphor of God as relational, many of our practiced modes of relating to God do not seem to fit. If God is relational in and through the web of life, God is not an other before whom we place ourselves. God is not the other to whom we direct our prayers. How do we relate to God the relation?

Praying and seeking the will of God take on a different character. If God is in our midst, if all is in God, if the universe is God's body, we are always in the presence of God. The world becomes then an altar. Breath provides channels of divine communication. Prayer becomes more a matter of attention and intention, than address to an other.

We do not pray for answers but for connection. We do not ask God to intervene, but we call on God's presence. We evoke God's companionship. We desire to have our intentions and God's be in harmony and work in concert.

In some ways the will of the relational God is very clear. We know what God wants, what God yearns for: mutual relationship, goodness, justice, love, and fullness of life. However, the specific application of God's will in any given circumstance is not given nor clearly knowable. What does justice mean in a particular instance? How do we know what will best enhance life? Therefore, we pray for discernment: not to know God's will so we can submit to it, but to perceive what shape the divine desire for life may take in the many complex and conflicted circumstances of life.

Since God's power is with us, we are the agents of God's will, not the objects of it. This does not mean we are in charge, able to control or determine the course of events. Nor do any of us operate autonomously. Rather, divine power is in all and all is in relation. In order to be true agents of God's will, we too must practice relationality and shared power in relation. We are to engage in mutually enhancing and interdependent relationships.

For some people these ideas find expression primarily in nature spirituality. These people seek to enter fully into connection with all of creation and thus to move more deeply into the web of life. For others, God is encountered in and through persons and social connections. They seek to live in loving and just relationships and to nurture community and sustaining societies. Whether the emphasis is on the natural world or on human society, faith is in relation. By embracing connection and being part of the web, we trust that God's will is being done, that the love and goodness of God are being made more manifest.

The Strengths of This Metaphor

In this world in which we are more and more aware of our interdependence, the metaphor of God as relational seems to make better sense than traditional notions of hierarchy and domination. We not only live within the World Wide Web that connects us technologically, but our lives are also shaped by multiple patterns of relation that are interdependent. A political crisis in the Middle East potentially affects us all, as does a viral epidemic in China. Physicists and ecologists have been teaching us that an event as seemingly insignificant as the beating of butterfly wings or as major as the destruction of a rain forest in one part of the globe can produce effects throughout the earth's systems.

The up and down linearity of a hierarchical universe does not fit with these realities of life today, including their complexity. The metaphor of a relational God is more suitable for our current consciousness and experiences, as is the idea that God's will is not directing and controlling.

We are expected to be adults in this world and relate to this God as adults. This, too, is a strength. Even though we human beings are not fully in charge of what happens in the world, we are responsible for our lives. When we behave as children, with the expectation that we will be taken care of or bailed out of whatever mess we find ourselves in, we leave it to others, often our children, to clean up after us. This is not fair.

The relational God reminds us of our responsibilities for and to life. This God's promise is not to take care of us, but to be there with and for us. Such companionship is an adult offer, in a relationship of mutuality.

We can no longer use God's will as an explanation for all that happens and that too is a strength, although it may not feel that way, especially for those accustomed to thinking of God's will as an explanation for the events of life. The relational God empowers us to act in accord with God's overall will for right relationship, justice, and well-being. We need to discern in any given set of circumstances how that will might be manifest and we need to act. God is present as companion and guide in the journey of faith. God's will does not control but empowers.

Although this view of God and God's will puts more emphasis on human responsibility for what happens in life, it does not assign blame to powerless victims. It does better with balancing power and responsibility, both for God and for human beings. Those who have the power to act are deemed more responsible for what happens.

Because God is present in and with the world in mutual relation, there is no clear division of labor between agent and recipient. As evidenced by the healing stories in the Gospels, power is present in the interaction between Jesus and those in need of healing. Jesus is also clear about not blaming those in need, the victimized. Rather it is the misdirected and evil powers that are the cause of distress and oppression. The relational God's will is aligned with good power, which some feminist theologians have described as erotic.

Yet another strength of this metaphor is that it pays more attention to creation. If the universe is God's body, then the created order manifests the divine and ought to be treated as such. When we abuse creation, we are harming God. Especially in today's world in which the future of the planet's ability to sustain life is increasingly threatened, care for the earth is an important value to emphasize.

The relational God is not gender specific. This God can be imaged as male or female, as friend or lover or companion or even mother in a nurturing and noncontrolling way. Because our lives contain a multitude of relationships, with men and women and the rest of creation, it makes sense to imagine God in multiple ways. When we do so we are less likely to think that any one of them corresponds absolutely to the being of God. We are more likely to recognize them as metaphors.

In Christianity the central truth of God is as Trinity. In traditional terms the Trinity is God the Father, the Son, and the Holy Spirit. Most often, in the past, thinking about the Trinity focused on the mystery of the three in one: how could three be one? What was the nature of their unity given that they had to be different and distinctive persons? However, if what is most true of God is relationality, if God is relation, then the Trinity expresses the reality that there is no God without relation, multiple relations. Relation is the heart, the essence, of the divine.

In that way the relational God witnesses to trinitarian truth and invites new interpretations of the Trinity. For example, Paul Fiddes offers a theology of the Trinity that is fully relational and participatory. For Fiddes, the persons of the Trinity, "Father" and "Son" and "Holy Spirit," are the relations, not persons in relationship or persons having relationships. The Trinity happens, so to speak, as movements of participation or to use the ancient term *perichoresis,* meaning coinherence or interbeing. Fiddes draws on the image of dance to represent the dynamism and participatory nature of this metaphor for Trinity. The emphasis is on the dance, not the dancers. The Trinity as dance is through movement, interaction, and participation. The community of faith joins in the dance and so enters into relation with God. It knows God through participation. Thus, this understanding of the Trinity leads to a more dynamic understanding not only of God but of human persons who are constituted through participation, movement, and connection.

The Limitations of This Metaphor

Those who criticize this metaphor for God do so from different angles and perspectives. Some would suggest that this God is too much like us, that there is not enough distinction between what God is like and who we are. In more theological language they would argue that God is not transcendent enough or that God's transcendence is diminished by bringing God too close. For example, when the church furniture gets rearranged so that everyone is facing one another, God becomes too familiar. When

God becomes too familiar, then we can too easily make God in our image and define God as we wish. In other words, instead of seeing this way of imagining God as a safeguard against forgetting that all our images of God are metaphors, these critics would argue the opposite.

It would seem then that such familiarity would also compromise the mystery of God. God's mystery has most often been a function of God's transcendence and otherness. We do not feel awe and wonder in relation to what we experience as familiar. The kind of feelings associated with companionship and friendship seem the opposite of those we attach to mystery, even though there is an awe and wonder to be known in and through intimacy. Nonetheless, there is a marked contrast between a church in the round and the vastness and soaring heights of a Gothic cathedral. It is the majestic dimension of God that is found lacking in this metaphor.

God's will is also lacking in a kind of strength. If God is not directly in charge, if God's will is not ultimately manifest, then there would seem to be little to comfort us, especially when we are experiencing violation or injustice. Is the relational God's presence as companion enough in such times of extreme need? Even the most able and responsible adults yearn at times to be taken care of, to find solace in strength beyond their own.

Thus far I have noted limitations of this metaphor that would be offered from the point of view of those whose God is likely to be found among the first several metaphors described in this book. There are critics, however, who think that the relational God does not go far enough in reimagining God.

One limitation such critics would highlight has to do with the goodness of God's power. We have seen how God's goodness or love and God's power may be in opposition or in tension in some expressions of God's will. This metaphor seeks to resolve the tension by making God's power a function of God's goodness and love. This is especially true of those who advocate for God's love as erotic power. Erotic power is good; it is opposed to bad uses of power that cause harm.

Understanding power in such terms perpetuates the moral dualism that has haunted Christian understandings of God and God's power. Such dualism maintains that in God's good universe, someone or something other than God has to be responsible for the introduction of evil, which remains totally other than God. The primary change that the proponents of this metaphor make to such a view has to do with moral valuation: That is, those things that were once deemed bad and even the source of evil, such as eros, sexuality, bodies, passion, and human willfulness, are now considered good. Indeed, they are of God. Thus moral dualism remains in place though its terms are altered.

This approach does not give due consideration to the nature of power, which cannot be confined to categories of good and bad. Nor does it account sufficiently for the complex and often unforeseen consequences of any action. Such consequences may effect outcomes neither desired nor chosen nor predicted. In other words, no willed action, no expression of agency, can be categorically good. Moral dualism diminishes our capacity to deal with the potentially contradictory and multiple outcomes of any action.

It also makes it difficult to account for the tragic dimensions of life. Tragedy often knows no direct agent: no one willed the harm directly. Such harm is the product of forces and processes unleashed unwittingly by human action or inaction or even outside of human and divine causation. Tragedy is a result of limitation and of circumstance.

Because traditional Christian thought was reluctant to attribute any limitation to God, it tended to banish tragedy from God's domain. But is not such limitation an aspect of relation, of being in relation? The question for those who embrace the relational God is whether they have made sufficient allowance for God's goodness to be touched by tragedy.

Finally, what we see in this metaphor is a desire to make God human, fully human, by expanding the personal images of God to embrace both genders and a variety of roles, especially ones that emphasize mutuality and partnership. As noted, advocates for the relational God, also put more emphasis on God's presence in, with, and through creation. Some see God as the power in relationship more than the person in relationship. In these ways this metaphor for God seems to be straining the limits of personal images of God but not breaking free of them. In the next chapter, we will consider a final way of understanding God that goes beyond imaging God as person.

8

POWER IN US

GOD AS ENERGY FOR LIFE

I N CHAPTER ONE I described a vision of God I had many years ago: the divine as flashes of light in motion, providing connection. I did not imagine God as a person but as energy, in dynamic interaction. This God had no face, nor a body. Most of us are so familiar and comfortable with personal images of God, whether we picture God as an old man with a long white beard sitting on a throne, or as a loving companion, walking alongside us in life, or as a caring mother, tenderly embracing us, that we can scarcely imagine God in any other way. At the time I had this vision, I myself did not know what to do with it. I had few resources for understanding it. In fact, I told no one about it because I assumed I would be dismissed or judged harshly.

My experience illustrates the challenges we face in imaging God as other than person and, more specifically, as energy. Are we willing and able to expand our imaginations to entertain ideas about God that may seem more unfamiliar than those we have encountered thus far? Is there an environment of openness and support for such envisioning? How do we encourage exploration?

This chapter focuses on a metaphor for God that is nonpersonal and abstract: God as energy for life. This God metaphor likens the divine to neither person nor concrete thing. Energy, by definition, is not matter. It is dynamism. Fundamentally, God as energy is force of life. God is action, rather than actor.

We are still in the world of metaphor. Even though God as energy for life does not have a face or personal attributes or even concrete features, any way we imagine God, whether abstract, concrete or personal, is metaphorical. Ultimately, it is an approximation of God, or even of what we know of God. However, this particular metaphor of God as energy for life allows us to imagine God in ways that more personal and concrete metaphors do not allow. It affords us different insight into the divine, as well as into the nature of the universe.

As I have already indicated, I find much value in this way of imaging God. Potentially, I see it as working better in our world today. It seems more consonant with the worldview of postmodernity, the findings of contemporary science, and the realities of life in a global and pluralistic society. For all those reasons it seems more appropriate and fitting than the hierarchical and even relational and person-centered metaphors we have explored thus far. This metaphor of divine energy does not privilege the human person as the supreme image of God. In that way it expands our perspective and may take us out of our human-centeredness. It also causes us to go beyond the familiar and everyday experiences of life and to see into the very heart of reality in a different way.

What Is Real

Metaphysics is that arena of thought that seeks to understand and explain the nature of reality. Metaphysical philosophers and theologians focus their attention on such questions as what is real? They have insisted that God is that which is the most real. A very common expression for this claim is that God is ultimate reality. What does this mean? There is no one answer to that question, but the variety of responses found in the Christian tradition share the belief that God is more real

than anything else. For some theologians and philosoph
means that everything that is not of God is in some way not re..
is not of God is lesser and perhaps untrue or illusory.

Strains of Christian thought, especially those most imbued with Greek philosophical ideas, hold that there is a unity at the heart of reality which is ultimately more real than the multiplicity and differences we all seem to experience in everyday life. The goal of faith then is union, to become one with the one. It is the one that is the most real, most true. The divine is the unity that is ultimate reality. Such ideas permeate not only Christian thought, but other religious traditions as well. For example, Buddhism talks about the veil of illusions that surround us in life. The path to enlightenment involves breaking through to find what is most real, to become one with all.

Still other strains of Christian thought emphasize God as supreme and ultimate. God's existence is categorically different from that of anything else or anyone. In fact, everything else derives from God, perhaps even reflects God but only as a pale shadow. God as the really real is not fully manifest in any finite being or thing. Another way to state this idea is to assert that we can only know reality partially in this life. As St. Paul states in 1 Corinthians 13:12: "For now we see in a mirror, dimly, but then we will see face to face."

How then are we to understand the character of this one and ultimate reality that is God? The twentieth-century Protestant theologian Paul Tillich, drawing on ancient traditions as well as modern ideas, thought that the essence of God, what is most real, is "being." For Tillich, God is the "ground of being." This means that everything that is, has being, or participates in being.

On one level, to be means to exist. To state that something has being is to suggest that it is. It has existence. But being is not just about the existence of things, it is also about the essence of things. Essence refers to nature of things, the nature of being. So being not only gives things existence, but it also makes them what they truly are and are meant to be. The common place term, "human being," connotes this idea: to be human means to have being, to be; but it also means to embody the character of humanness, to "be" in a particular way.

As the ground of being, God is both the source of all that exists and also the purpose or essence of what is. The goal of faith for Tillich is to participate as fully in being as possible. By becoming most truly one's essence, a being exists more truly in relation to the divine as ground of being.

Tillich was not alone in thinking about God in these ways. However abstract it may sound to image God as source of life or ground of being or the end our essence seeks, these ideas speak of the power of God as that which makes life happen and which enlivens our existence. Roman Catholic theologian Karl Rahner drew upon such approaches to talk about the nature of God and to imagine Jesus as the being in whom existence and essence converge fully. For Rahner, Jesus lived and died in such a way that he fulfilled what Rahner termed his *obediential potency*, the ability to actualize the divine presence and realize being. Rahner understood such living to be characterized by openness to mystery that is divinity.

Tillich and Rahner have both found resources in ancient traditions, rooted in Greek philosophical traditions. For early church theologians who used the language of being to describe God, the character of being was static. As we have discussed, God, being itself, did not—and could not—change. God's being remained constant eternally. Neither Tillich nor Rahner, however, understand being as static or given. For them being has a dynamic aspect as becoming; there is development in human life, in history, and in creation.

Such development, the process of becoming, has a goal. As determined by its essence or nature, any being has an end for which God created it. God wills the fulfillment or actualization of that end. By living in obedience and faithfulness to their essence, beings are fulfilling God's will. For example, in Rahner's theology, Jesus Christ is the actualization of being because he is living in full obedience to his divine essence.

The goal remains constant: for all beings to fulfill the possibility built into existence and being by God, the creator and source of all. What gets in the way and thwarts such fullness of being are sin and the consequences of sin. According to Christian teaching, through redemption, realized through Jesus' life, death, and resurrection, sin is defeated. Redemption means that which was lost because of sin is reclaimed. Human beings can still realize their God-given potential through grace.

Imagining God as being itself or as ultimate reality begins to take us out of the realm of a personal God. These perspectives also let us view life as a dynamic process throughout creation. Because all life forms have being, theologies of being make room for the array of God's creation in the scope of God's will. Each and every thing is potentially becoming and growing into the fullness of its being.

In these theological approaches, God, the divine, is the really real. God, as being itself or the ground of being, is the source and end of life. We are not fully ourselves, not living into what we can be, until we come to know and be one with God as the true goal and end of life. The more we realize that end, the closer life comes to fullness of being.

No matter how dynamically or existentially these theologies understand being, they maintain a notion of God's being and purpose as fixed. There is a God-given end to existence which fixes how being ought to be realized. In that sense, God precedes, determines, and completes all that God intends.

From Essence to Energy

If we image God as energy, then we imagine the heart of reality, what is most real, as energy. Energy is the dynamic, driving force within all that exists. It is potential and possibility, power and movement. Energy is ever in motion and indeterminate. It is not observable in and of itself. When scientists study energy or try to measure energy, what they perceive and observe are its effects or interactions.

One of the effects or manifestations of energy which scientists observe is light. Coincidentally, light is a common metaphor for the divine. God is light; the divine enlightens. Prayers and hymns name God as light. Jesus is extolled as the light of the world. The Holy Spirit enlightens minds and hearts. Light as a metaphor for God captures a key aspect of the divine as that which opens up possibilities, guides our way, and lifts our spirits. Light allows us to see what is hidden and therefore unknown. It also gives warmth. Light is a way God as energy is manifest, as well as that by which God is known.

Much of what we know about energy and the nature of reality as energy comes from quantum physics. It offers a way to imagine reality as energy. As discussed in chapter one, Albert Einstein effected a revolution in modern physics and in our understanding of reality by thinking differently about the relationship of energy and matter. His famous formula, $E = mc^2$, suggests that everything is ultimately energy, that matter converts to energy when it reaches a certain speed. In addition, his theory of relativity pointed to the lack of separation of what had been taken to be distinct building blocks of the universe: space and time. Ultimately, everything is interrelated; everything affects everything else.

Though Einstein's ideas are now a hundred years old, they are still mind bending. How are we to make sense of the idea that energy is the really real? Or that space and time are a continuum? In our day-to-day life, we live in a very different world, a world of materiality. We plot location and measure time. Our commonplace assumption is that the world we live in is fixed. We view things as substantive. So, for example, the chair on which I sit and the computer on which I write consist of matter, which is concrete and inert. How then are we to imagine the chair and the computer as really consisting of energy, dynamic energy, ever in motion? What does it mean to assert that what is most real about my chair is that it is ultimately and fundamentally energy?

Einstein's ideas and the findings of some physicists who came before him and many who came after him lead us precisely to this conclusion. The universe and everything in it is energy. In the beginning and in the end is energy.

Physicists provide other key ideas about the nature of reality that hold important meaning for how we imagine God. One is implied in the equation $E = mc^2$: namely, that nothing is ever lost. Matter converts to energy. Energy forms into matter. But in the process, there is no loss, only change. Might not this scientific principle offer a way to imagine the redemptive process?

Because energy is dynamic, ever changing and causing change, what is most real about the universe is dynamism and change. Change is fundamental to reality. Nothing is fixed. Nothing remains the same. Change is also constant. The universe is anything but static. It is alive as pulsating, continuous motion.

Such motion is multidirectional as well as constant. Multiplicity, not oneness, is sign of the real. Difference is one way that multiplicity manifests. The rich variety of creation is evidence of this aspect of divine energy.

Such motion is also connecting, making whatever happens happen, but not in any way that is fixed or given. What follows then is that the really real is ultimately indeterminate. Indeterminacy suggests that there is no inherent directionality or directing purpose. There is no determinism. Chance and chaos are built into existence.

This universe of energy is what makes life happen. What is fundamental to life, what is the really real, is pulsating, interacting, interrelating movement. There is, however, no given end built into existence other than life itself. Life is open, the future open ended. There is no fixed essence or even existence that is particular to the life of any given thing.

We might think of such energy as the life force of the universe. Its power is of and for life. If we can speak of any directing purpose, it is for life. The universe keeps going, both in the sense of constant motion and dynamism but also in the sense that life seeks life. Life is ongoing.

Despite theories that purport the universe is moving toward extinction, there seems to be a fundamental drive for existence, for living, that asserts itself again and again, even in the bleakest and most dire of circumstances. Suns die out in one galaxy, but new suns form in another. Within a blackened landscape, the product of a forest fire, we can see new green growth emerge, seemingly from ashes. Human beings survive the worst of brutal violence and go on with their lives.

Life seeking life, however, may also mean that species die out. No particular life, no thing, is forever. Constant evolution is the state of the universe and seems to be at the heart of reality. Life as a whole goes on, changing and evolving.

Divine Energy rather than Will

What happens to our image of God if the divine is understood to be energy for life? What difference would it make if God were not a being, but energy as the really real that makes life happen? What if ultimate reality were energy, ever in motion and indeterminate?

The divine as energy for life is not fixed in any way. This means that we not only need to recognize that what we say about God is metaphor and does not correspond directly to who God is and so is subject to change, but also that the divine itself is changing and so not determined or given. God as energy is ever in motion and flux.

In this view of God, change is not only a part of God, but it is the very nature of the divine. What is most true of God is constant dynamism, as was the case in my vision of points of light, ever moving. Such motion does not pursue a set direction, a given path. It is indeterminate.

However, the dynamic motion of God as energy is not totally random. We can speak of purpose to the extent that God as energy enables life. The purpose of divine power, as energy, is life. The divine energizes into existence. God is the energy of and for life.

Though divine energy is life producing, it does not direct life in any given way or toward a given end. God as energy cannot be said to have a will per se. The notion of will, as we commonly think of it, does not even fit because will is a human attribute. Willing connotes directed intent, even determination. It would seem to be the opposite of the indeterminacy and nondirecting dynamism of God as energy.

Thus God as energy does not will what happens in our lives, nor in nature, other than to energize for life. The power of God, which is the energy of God, is what makes life and living possible, resilient and ongoing. However, God as energy does not direct nor will what happens in the world to happen. This God is not an agent.

Immanence and Transcendence

Is this God as energy for life immanent or transcendent? On one level this view of God may seem radically immanent. If God is energy for life then God is in everything. God is present everywhere. Nothing and no one has life without the presence of God. Metaphors of God as breath or life force or even heart connote this. Just as we are not alive without the presence of breath or a beating heart, if we are alive then God is with us and in us. The divine is present not only in us, but in all that is alive, the whole universe and all that is in it. God is in creation, all of it. This is full panentheism. It may even be a form of pantheism since everything and everyone is fundamentally energy.

Yet, just as matter and energy are related but cannot be collapsed one into the other, this God is not like us. God is especially not like the way we most commonly experience ourselves and our lives. So we can also say that God as energy is fully transcendent, totally other than us, precisely because God does not exist like anything that we know exists.

In that way God as energy for life is mystery, incomprehensible to our limited abilities of perception and cognition. God is as close as breath yet beyond the universe. God is the power of life but not contained by any and all life. If we are living, we know and experience God. Yet if we are honest, we confess we apprehend but a hint of this divine power.

At the heart of the mystery of God is life. Why is there life at all? Is not the presence of the universe a mystery beyond all imagining? Even with the increasing ability of scientists to explain the origins of the universe and to imagine and even predict its future, the presence and abundance, rich variety and amazing complexity of life in all its forms is a wonder to behold. In truth, we can behold but a small fraction of it. We can sense but a tremor of the immense power of life.

Some of the traditional attributes of God take on new meaning when read through the image of God as energy for life. For example, the idea that God is immortal and eternal. For early church theologians, God's immortality meant that God did not change. God's being as eternal was in no way affected by change. But immortal and eternal can also mean that God is life unending. Just as energy is never lost but only changes forms, the divine power that is life remains and endures.

Ultimately the notions of immanence and transcendence seem to strain at their definitional seams, especially when they are held to be opposites. Just as we now know matter and energy are in relationship and fundamentally united, immanence and transcendence are perhaps best understood in relation. What happens if we look at yet another pair of traditional attributes of God through the lens of God as energy?

Beyond Moral Dualism

Throughout this book, we have discussed the relationship of power and goodness in God. We have looked at the various ways in which God's power and goodness, manifest as love, have been defined. Most often those speaking for the Christian tradition have wanted to maintain both God's power and goodness. Yet because suffering and other problematic realities of life tend to set those in opposition, much theological effort has gone into the relationship of God's power and goodness. Patriarchal and hierarchical images of God affirmed God's power as good. God's love was demonstrated through God's power, no matter what the human costs. As we turned to more relational views of God and ones that paid attention to suffering as a fundamental challenge to God's goodness and/or God's power, we saw movement toward redefining God's power as noncontrolling, as self-limiting, and as expressed in vulnerability and suffering love.

However, God's goodness is rarely challenged, especially in modernity. The majority of theologians, be they process, liberation, political, relational, or creation theologians, are more willing and able to redefine God's power than to question God's goodness. They are more likely to propose that God's power is limited than to imagine God as anything other than love. In some measure this is due to the moral dualism that has been at the heart of Christian thought and that has equated God with goodness.

By definition any worldview is limited. It is one standpoint, a particular way of seeing and understanding what one sees. A worldview based on moral dualism allows us to see and interpret the world in certain ways only. It does not permit and even precludes other perspectives that may cast a different light on life and what happens in it. In order to begin to entertain other perspectives, we need to question not only the dualism of this traditional worldview but the presumption that the universe and God are to be understood as moral.

This may seem an especially provocative and problematic assertion. How could God not be moral? How could God not be good? Even such questions belie a worldview, a particular perspective on God. Attributes such as "moral" and "good" tend to be ascribed to persons and personal agents. If God is not person, if the divine does not act agentially, then what is the meaning of such attributes? In what sense can we talk about energy as moral or even good?

God as energy is not moral as we generally understand that term. Categories of good and evil cannot be applied straightforwardly to energy. The worldview of moral dualism does not work in the world of energy. It uses a different language, a foreign language, that cannot be translated in a way that fits or even makes sense if all is energy.

Those of us embedded in a worldview of moral dualism may well recoil from such ideas. We are so used to thinking in terms of putting everything into categories of good and evil, that if someone suggests that God is not good, then our immediate response is to think that makes God evil, and that just cannot be. God cannot be evil. Such an idea is beyond the pale for most people.

However, such reasoning remains within the terms set by moral dualism: God has to be good or evil. A dualistic framework only recognizes those choices as valid. I am suggesting that if we step out of that worldview, truly step out of it, then we will no longer use those terms when talking about God. We will not necessarily describe God with the language of good and evil nor will we attribute the things that happen in our lives to God's moral agency and will.

What does this mean for the nature of God as energy? In what ways might we imagine God in relation to goodness and power? Is it possible to talk about what God does? I have already suggested that we can imagine God as energy as having a kind of intent. The inclination of that intent is for life, to enable life, and keep life going. It may follow then that goodness and even love, as ascribed to God, are functions of God as source and energy for life. In other words, it is not so much that God loves, since love is a human, and perhaps animal, emotion, but we can say that the life that God as energy makes possible is experienced as love. Life cannot continue without nurture and care and so an effect, an outcome, of God's intent for life is the presence of love and care in the universe. God is not good per se, but because we experience life as a good thing and God as energy makes life possible, we perceive God as good. We are glad to be alive, glad to be part of the universe. We give thanks to the God of life.

The perspective I am proposing has roots in the biblical view of God. In the story of creation in Genesis, when God looked upon creation and declared it good, this was not a moral judgment. God was not declaring that since God is morally good, everything that God makes reflects that goodness nor that creation's behavior was good as opposed to evil. Rather God's naming creation as good meant that it was fitting. God's voiced judgment was an aesthetic one, a comment of appreciation, even of enjoyment. It is good that creation exists, just as it is good to be alive. Creation as the product of divine energy is to be valued and appreciated.

Energy as Power

Energy may not be morally good, but it is powerful and strong. In fact, energy is power. The dynamism of energy is powerful. Since energy is at the core of all that is, we might even say it is absolute power. Such power, the dynamism of energy, is not moral, however.

This, too, is an unfamiliar concept for many of us. Even when it comes to power, the moral dualism inherent in our common worldview is difficult to overcome. We tend to think in terms of good power and bad power. Some people hold the view that power is inherently bad or corrupting.

Others differentiate between what is good power and what is bad power, often by what the power makes happen. Power can be used for good or evil. Scores of films, such as the *Star Wars* series, play out this premise. Power used for evil harms, abuses, and destroys. Power used for good makes life better.

We also think of power most often as a possession: The powerful have power; the powerless do not. As we saw with the metaphors of God as monarch or patriarch, God is the most powerful, which means God has the most power, if not all the power.

Power, however, is neither moral, nor is it a thing, a possession. Power is potential energy. It is motion. Such energy may cause harm or do good along the way, but its nature is neither. Most often both harm and good are outcomes of the dynamism of power and sometimes such outcomes cannot be discerned or easily identified.

Imagine a river that makes life possible for those who live along it. The river provides water for drinking and eating and washing. It also waters plants and helps vegetation to grow. The water may provide transportation so that a journey of days can be made much shorter by going with the flow of the current, as the energy and power of water carries passengers along.

Imagine also the power of a raging river, causing destruction all along its path, as it rips out bushes and even upends trees on its banks and as it isolates and strands people who are no longer able either to traverse its waters or draw upon its resources. Would we call the raging river evil or bad? Would we call the gently flowing river good?

The river simply is being a river, its own power, dynamism, and nature in interaction with the atmosphere and weather and other factors of terrain and environment. The river is ever changing, ever in motion. Its intent, if we can speak of intent, is to flow, to be river. Harm is not intended, but it does happen.

Christianity has tended to domesticate God and to make God a moral agent so that the raw power of divinity, perhaps we may even say the wild side of God, seems unimaginable and even blasphemous. Yet anyone who spends time in the wilderness or even draws back to observe the broad sweep of history cannot think of the world, and life in it, as gentle or kind or always good. The Christian answer to the presence of harm has most often been sin. The harshness of life is the result of sin, which in turn is the result of human disobedience and faithlessness. God, however, is the opposite of sin in a dualistic worldview and so not party to the harmful and savage aspects of life.

God as energy is like a river rather than a moral agent. The power of God as energy just is. This power makes life possible and enables life to go on, but the indeterminacy of the universe, the complexity of life in creation, and the multitude of interactions of life in human society result in what are experienced as clashes and conflicts, failures and disasters that cause harm and death for species, societies, and even civilizations. It is fitting to work against such forces and outcomes. It is helpful to build in safeguards where and when we can: to build bridges perhaps and store water so even when the river is not accessible, life along its banks is not so easily disrupted. But we cannot ultimately or fully rid ourselves or the world of what results in harm. Life endures, but it is also ever challenged. Such is the nature of reality.

There is no final victory as promised in the dualistic worldview. There is no completion. The future remains open ended. In contrast, Christian portrayals of a last judgment or an apocalypse play out the final victory. These witness to the measure of God's power and goodness. The assurance of a final victory suggests that, although God's goodness may seem to be losing out in the moment or even across the sweep of history, God will win out in the end. God's power is capable of restoring all that has been lost. No seeming triumph of evil is final. Such narratives seek assurances against the indeterminacy and complexity of life.

Those who wrote the books of the New Testament thought in terms of powers and principalities that inhabited and acted in the world. Even though those writers were operating within a dualistic worldview, their world was not domesticated. It was alive with powers and forces that buffeted people about and to which people and even the created order were vulnerable. Energies of all kinds were loosed in the universe. Finding ways to navigate among them and even manage life with them became a focus of religious attention. Divine energy provided strength and power in that process.

Some indigenous religions view the world in similar ways. For them, all life forms contain spirits that both help and hinder human beings. The world, the whole world and everything in it, is alive for the adherents of these religions. In that way these indigenous religions perceive energy as the heart of reality more clearly than the so-called higher religions do. They also recognize that such energy can be violent as well as caring. Religious practices enable participants to relate to these spirits in such a way that life is managed and enhanced. For example, Native American smudging rituals cleanse and seek to bring practitioners into right relation with the spirits in a place. Other rituals are meant to bring energies into better balance.

The rituals of Christianity may not be all that different. The story that accompanies them may speak in terms of sin and redemption, of praise and thanksgiving, of petition and intercession, but fundamentally the rituals, such as communion or baptism, confession or anointing, intend to bring the faithful into right relation with the power of God. The Christian story, as I have argued, subjects God's power to a dualistic framework, but the need to relate to that power in a way that enables life, even in raw form, still energizes the rituals.

So rather than seeking to do God's will, it is more fitting to speak of connecting with the power of God as energy and strength for life. Such power is like the raging river, as well as the flowing stream. It destroys, even as it creates. Destruction does not make God evil, nor does creation make God good. Both destruction and creation are part of an ongoing process of life. Life leads to death; death flows back to life. In the world of energy there is no ultimate loss, but there is constant change. All is in motion, life unto life.

Prayer and Worship

What does it mean to pray to God when God is not a person? How does such a God hear us and respond to us? How are we to worship such a God? Most of us are so used to prayer as a type of dialogue, even if God does not respond directly, that we can scarcely imagine prayer in any other form. And we are likely to view worship as a group conversation or drama directed toward God, who is also actor and director. What happens to prayer and worship when God is energy? Are prayer and worship still possible or recognizable?

I have already hinted that many rituals are fundamentally about connecting with the power of God. Ultimately, the narratives and dramatic actions of any ritual are simply expressions of the desire to connect. They function as vehicles of relationship. Christians gather around a table and share bread and wine. Buddhists chant or sit in silent meditation for hours. In some religions adherents burn incense and dance. In others they fast or immerse themselves in cleansing water. They also simply breathe, in and out, bringing their attention and breath into harmony with the universe. Whatever the ritual, the purpose and goal is to connect with the divine, to be in relationship with what is considered really real.

Prayer, worship, ritual are fundamentally "energy work." They are the motion, the points of light I imagined, making connection, bringing into relationship, changing configuration, and making life happen. Our worship, whatever form it takes, is about focusing energy and participating in the relation of all.

Forms of meditation and contemplation are particularly fitting for this type of energy work since often they are about connecting with energy or channeling it. These practices do not require God, as an other, to whom one addresses prayer. Meditation may well bring us more into communion with God. Contemplation may immerse us in dynamic interrelationships. Both may help us be more aware of life and the energy that makes life possible. In that way, they bring us closer to the divine, without necessarily addressing God directly.

Some scientists have been arguing that prayer helps people heal, even if those who are ill do not ask for the prayers or even know that they are being prayed for. If God is energy for life and prayer is about connecting with the divine energy, then there is a way in which healing can be "energized" or "mobilized" by prayer. God is not an agent in this scenario who is directing the action or choosing who gets healed or not. Rather God is the energy that configures or not in such a way that healing in enabled. The person who is the recipient of healing may well need to be open and receptive to the changes of energy, but not necessarily with direct knowledge of the prayers of others.

Since everything is interrelated and everything affects everything else, change is always happening, energy is constantly moving and producing effects. Our actions, even our breathing, move energy, whether we are conscious of the movement or not. Prayer and worship involve paying attention to that energy in a way we do not in every moment of our lives. Those who practice spiritual disciplines are often attempting to have such consciousness and attention become more constant in their lives.

Many years ago, during a two-week residential workshop I was attending, some of the participants, including myself, decided to spend time during the weekend sharing various spiritual practices with which we were familiar. We came together as a group of virtual strangers, with all the defenses folks might bring to new encounters. Early on in our time together we chanted the simple Hindu syllable of "om." Our chanting lasted perhaps twenty or thirty minutes. Afterwards we fell into conversation that included a deep level of sharing, even of personal revelation. One member of our group whom a number of us had experienced as particularly closed and defended seemed especially open.

Something had happened through the chanting to connect and bring us closer to one another, more so than hours of conversation might have. Perhaps our chanting moved energy to create relationship, ground trust, and help us be at ease with one another. It rendered the spaces among us not ones of separation, but of connection.

In truth, connection is happening all the time, even through the routine activities of daily life, such as eating with one's family, playing with a child, worshiping with one's home congregation, working at a job, or walking in the woods. Energy is released even if we are not paying attention as we might. There is a subtle and cumulative effect of such energy work that the monastic traditions of combining work and prayer have long understood. Occasionally, even the most mundane of activities is experienced in an immensely powerful or deeply moving way. Then the everyday becomes transformative. In those moments, something happens that is more than the sum of the parts. Divine energy manifests in a different kind of way.

Experiences of divine energy, however they happen, leave us feeling more alive and thankful for life. We know that we are part of a whole, something more than ourselves. Those moments offer evidence of the power of God as energy for life. They reveal the mystery that is life. They evoke our wonder.

Metaphoric Play

Because the concept of energy is so abstract and so difficult to hold in our imaginations, we may seek ways to give energy form. There are several traditional images of God that approximate the characteristics of God as energy. One I have already discussed is light.

The image of God as light was especially popular among early church theologians. For them, however, light was opposed to darkness, within a dualistic worldview. Light was equated with the good and, therefore, with God and darkness with evil. Light was the source of enlightenment and salvation; darkness connoted ignorance and condemnation.

If God is energy, however, light is not opposed to darkness, so much as related to it. As Psalm 139, addressing God, states: "darkness and light to you are both alike." We can view both as dimensions of the divine.

What makes light such an appropriate metaphor is that it is a manifestation of energy. Light is dynamic. Although scientists have argued that light is a wave or a particle, most have come to view it as neither. Rather what seem to be particles or waves are effects of light. Light itself remains indefinable and indeterminate.

We do know that the effects of light provide illumination as well as heat. In those ways, light enables life. Other forms of light, such as sunlight, also seem to point to the dynamic and life-giving qualities of God. They also gesture to the ways in which encountering the divine holds a certain danger.

Another metaphor for energy is life. Life is also a common way to understand God. God is life itself or the source of life. Since life is still abstract, there are a number of metaphorical ways to image life, such as water or air or breath. God is like water, which makes life possible. God is like air or breath without which no one can live.

Perhaps the most "personified" image of God as energy is spirit. The Spirit is one of the "persons" of the Trinity in Christianity and has traditionally been understood as the dynamic power of connection and relationship. Spirit is the energy of the divine: creating, transforming, and empowering. The Spirit itself has traditional images associated with it, such as a bird/dove or wind or fire. These connote freedom as well as strength. The Spirit blows where it wills; it manifests divine presence. Images of the Spirit point to the dynamic, ever moving quality of divine energy that is the source of life. In that sense the Spirit can be imagined as laboring and giving birth. It is ever-making life happen.

Hymns to the Spirit give voice to its qualities:

> O Holy Spirit, by whose breath
> life rises vibrant out of death;
> come to create, renew, inspire;
> come kindle in our hearts your fire. . . .

> Praise the Spirit in creation,
> breath of God, life's origin:
> Spirit, moving on the waters,
> quickening worlds to life within,
> source of breath to all things breathing,
> life in whom all lives begin.

The Strengths of This Metaphor

God as energy for life celebrates, values, and honors life as a dynamic process in which everyone and everything participates. In the beginning and end is life. The whole universe is alive, as is everything in it. Divine energy animates all.

This universe is a pulsing web of relations. The emphasis here is on interrelationship, interdependence, and dynamic connection. Everything is in relation with and affects everything else. Human beings are part of the web of creation. We are no longer the center of the universe nor are we the pinnacle of a hierarchy. Rather everything that is manifests God as the energy for life.

The interconnection of all recognizes and honors the diversity of creation, as well as its processes of life and death, from the level of microorganisms to that of galaxies. The driving force of the universe is life ongoing. Nothing is lost in creation, but nothing remains the same. This view allows for reimagining traditional concepts such as resurrection and eternal life, not as the continuation of distinct selves as ego centers, but as transformation into energy for life.

Understanding God as energy is more consonant with what we know today, from scientists and others, about the nature of the universe and how it works. God as energy fits with quantum theory as does interconnectivity as the expression of that energy. Just as metaphors of monarchy and patriarchy made sense in and reflected the ancient and premodern world, images of God as energy connect with the scientific world of today.

They are also more fitting for the socially global and religiously pluralistic world we inhabit. Energy is everywhere and can take many forms. Divine energy may be manifest in and through a variety of religious expressions. The "truth" of Christianity shares the stage with other religions. Understanding God as energy makes it possible to relate to and appreciate the rituals and expressions of other religions, each with its own way to connect with divine energy.

God as energy also has the potential to equalize power, since everything that has life participates in energy and the power of energy. If power is dynamism, then power is a function of systems. Amassing power is like clogging up the pipes so that the power cannot flow, but is directed to and kept in one location. Transformation is accomplished by freeing up the flow of power. Many ethical affirmations about liberation, equality, and justice may be derived from understanding power in this way.

Freedom, justice, and equality are important values, not because they are good as opposed to evil but because they make life possible. Life begets life in a regenerating universe. Human existence is more alive, more whole, when these values are lived out. In that sense freedom and justice produce life.

God as energy also has the capacity to reawaken a sense of wonder and to reconnect with God as mystery. Such mystery evokes within us a mystical apprehension of the relatedness of all that is, along with a sense of the profound complexity of life and our inability to fathom it in its fullness.

Finally, I would suggest that imagining God as energy is closer to the nature of the divine than those metaphors that image God with human characteristics. The divine more closely resembles and is more truly energy than person.

The Limitations of This Metaphor

Most people prefer to relate to a personal God. God as energy for life seems too abstract, too unknowable, too unimaginable. It feels too impersonal. When we pray, we want an "other" to address. Even images of light or spirit remain too abstract.

From this chief limitation flow several others. For those seeking comfort or support, a God of indeterminacy and constant motion may seem too challenging or even disturbing. Especially in times of need, many of us prefer to imagine God's loving embrace or even the solidity of God as rock.

If we view God as energy, the question arises: do we not lose the specificity of Christian images of God and especially the Christian emphasis on incarnation and materiality? I would argue that understanding God as energy lends itself easily to fresh reinterpretations of central Christian concepts, but others might disagree.

They also question how biblically based a view of God as energy is. Although there are resources in the Bible for imagining God as energy, these are far fewer than other images of God, especially those that see God as person. More resources might be found in the theological and philosophical traditions, but even then there is a need, as I have argued, to shift from views of being as static and unchanging to fully dynamic perspectives on existence.

Yet others would argue that the goodness of God is essential to Christianity and a form of moral dualism is necessary to viewing God as good. They would find the emphasis on power, especially as it is redefined, theologically and ethically problematic. God's power has to be good. Any other understanding of God means that God is not God.

A related concern would be the nondirectionality of divine action. If God does not will, if everything is indeterminate, then are we not all simply adrift in the world, with nothing to count on and nothing to guide our way? Guide may be the key word here. How can God as indeterminate, dynamic energy guide us when we are looking for answers and for direction?

This metaphor for the divine might also breed a type of ethical passivity. Should we not accept whatever life offers us if there is no direction or ultimate resolution to guide our way? How are we to discern and know when to accept things and when to act? On what basis would we make ethical judgments and take action?

If God does not will or if God's will is not directing, and if God's nature is not given, the foundations that many have counted on for support and direction, including for ethical action, seem to be gone. Although the lack of foundations is consonant with a postmodern worldview, it is disconcerting for many people. How can God be God if God is not in charge? It seems unimaginable.

Perhaps that is the fundamental limitation of this image of God: It is so different from what many of us have been schooled in for most of our lives. We may find it difficult to imagine the divine in this way and that may well makes us uneasy. Incorporating God as energy into our lives, our worship and our way of being in the world may present quite a challenge.

Having moved through a range of metaphors for God, from monarch through several parental and relational images, to God as energy, certain questions could well be asked of any of these perspectives. What difference does any given metaphor make for how we live our lives? How are we to find our way amid the variety of metaphors? The next and final chapter will address such questions.

EPILOGUE

FOR THE LIVING

REIMAGING GOD

WHEN I EXPERIENCED GOD AS ENERGY, represented as connecting, interacting points of light in motion, I told no one about it. I wonder what would have happened if I had spoken about it then and shared my image with the woman who believed God to be father in a hierarchical and tiered universe. How would she have responded? And the other folks at the gathering, how might they have heard what I recounted? Would any of them have been able to receive my image with openness and curiosity? I feared they would not, especially since I myself did not know what to do with it at the time. I was unsure of my own experience, my own envisioning. That is why I kept it to myself and even from myself.

I no longer have such a sense of caution. I now know that very many people—faithful, honest, intelligent people—experience God in a wide variety of ways. They have rich images and profound insights to share. Hearing about these and so developing more awareness of the different ways in which people encounter God might enrich everyone's understanding of God.

Perhaps that would have been true thirty or so years ago as well. If I had shared my vision, maybe someone in the group would have said: "Yes, I know what you mean. Here's a way I imagine God that seems similar." Or others would have said: "Hmm, we never thought about God that way, but tell us more. Let's explore it together." My fear, however, was that they would not have understood and would have disapproved.

That fear was rooted in the way the images of God as father and lord and of the universe as hierarchical were so often presented as God-given truth. They were God's revelation, deposited, so to speak, by God in scripture and in the teachings and traditions of the church. Within this view of revelation, scripture and tradition contain certain knowledge of the nature and will of God, as communicated by those who hold authority in the church. Such knowledge is not open to question.

In this book I have been arguing for a different way to understand what we know about God. All such knowledge is an approximation. It arises from experiences and takes shape through language and imagination. The language we use to speak about God is metaphorical. What we say about God is rooted in imagination, our own imaginations, as well as those of people throughout history who have passed on their insights. Scripture and the teachings of the churches are the repositories of the experiences, imagination and knowledge of those who have gone before us. They convey the interplay between experience, imagination and thinking, personal and communal.

Alongside them, we have the work of visual artists and iconographers and the words of poets and mystics who enrich the pool of available metaphors. Whether we turn to the poetry of the Hebrew prophets or of contemporary writers, whether we gaze upon the ceiling of the Sistine Chapel or a painting of Our Lady of Guadalupe, we are encountering someone's apprehension of the divine.

As we have seen, experiences of the divine and the metaphors used to express them do not occur in a vacuum. They happen in particular times and places, in particular cultural contexts. Those social settings shape and give form to awareness of God. They both feed people's imaginations and set limits on them. As cultural contexts change, either over time or by the encounter with different cultures, people's imaginations change as well. They are then able to imagine new and different things. In turn, what they, and we, think about God also changes.

All these images of God we encounter help us grasp the ungraspable, fathom the unfathomable. God is like them, but is not equivalent to them. We struggle to know more fully, more authentically. Even then, we hold what we know of God like grains of sand in our hands. Such knowledge seems to slip through our fingers as we try to hold on to it.

The divine overwhelms us. Knowledge of God is inexhaustible, more than all the grains of sand on all the beaches on all the planets. We behold it only in part and through haze, much as heat waves shimmer above the sands and the glare of sun causes us to squint, distorting perception. But we behold it nonetheless.

Discernment

Given that what we know of God remains partial and approximate, how do we discern what to embrace? How do we determine what to eschew because it might lead us in problematic directions? How do we assess what we say about God and the metaphors we use for God?

A measure of our knowledge of God, as I have indicated, is whether it is life-giving. If God is power for life, redeeming life, then who God is and who we are in relation to God should foster and produce life. The meaning of redemption is such life, lived fully and abundantly. Abundant life is lived best if it includes justice and care, peace and well-being.

Life is also the evaluative principle by which knowledge of God is discerned and measured. Only that which enhances life need command our full allegiance. Key questions of discernment follow from this evaluative principle: What is the potential for life? What is more life-giving and sustaining of life for all—not only for an individual, but for a community, the world and creation itself? Questions to ask of any metaphor for God include: Does this metaphor foster life? Does what is attributed to God enhance life? Does this way of understanding God and the world support the life of the world?

Any of the metaphors we have considered might potentially be meaningful. As we have seen, all of them are able to claim roots in scriptural and theological traditions. We might find resources for exploring any of them further in the writings of faithful people throughout the centuries of the church's life. The question remains, however, whether they work, so to speak, in our day, in our context, to enhance and deepen and renew life.

Ultimately, that question has to be asked and answered again and again in every circumstance. The answer is always context specific and always complex. It requires discernment.

Cultural Context and Discernment

In exploring the way in which religion functioned in particular cultural contexts, the anthropologist Clifford Geertz pointed out that religions produce "moods and motivations" among their adherents. Those moods and motivations, in turn, direct and shape the lives of adherents. Such adherents live in particular ways, according to the worldview of the religion.

In many cultures, times, and places, especially before the modern era, religious, social, and cultural systems were so interconnected and such givens in people's lives, that they did not actively choose what they would believe nor how they would live. Today, in western society in particular, choice—and the importance of personal choice—is so embedded in our culture and its ideologies, that our commitment to religion is viewed as a voluntary association, something we choose because it holds value for us. Yet vestiges of the past remain. Many of us live in an interplay between "old world" thinking about religion as a given and modernity's emphasis on personal choice. That is our cultural inheritance and it shapes our responses to religion.

Ultimately, discernment—whether it entails making a choice or following a prescribed path—is always done within a cultural context that produces moods and motivations and shapes the way people think and act. The question of what is life-giving, sustaining, and fulfilling is not something that is the same in all times and places. Knowledge of God as life-giving wisdom is culturally produced, apprehended, and appreciated. For example, biblical scholars are quick to tell us that in order to understand the biblical message, we need to explore the cultural context that produced it and the meanings the text had in that context. Then we need to be able to "translate" it and relate it to our current context.

In today's global village conflicting forces shape our social and cultural contexts. On the one hand, we are more aware of, and even participate in, the multiplicity of cultures and the differences among cultures. When I was growing up, the only ethnic food my family ate, other than our own Armenian cuisine, was spaghetti. Now, in any given week, I may have food from four or five different cultures: Italian, Chinese, Indian, Mexican, as well as Armenian and American.

On the other hand, globalization, especially as expressed through a capitalist economic system, tends to eliminate difference. The worldwide presence of McDonald's or Coca Cola, including their iconic symbols, offers evidence of homogeneity. Wherever we go, we can look for the golden arches and get a hamburger and a Coke.

Culture also changes. It may be safe to say that change is the one constant of life and society. When I look back over my own lifetime, I am aware of immense changes. I still remember the introduction of television. My family's first television was more cabinet than screen. All the shows we watched were in black and white. There were three, maybe four, channels available. Now televisions are mounted flat against the wall, black and white viewing is vintage, and cable companies tout the availability not only of an immense number of channels but of online viewing menus. I was over thirty before I first used a computer, but many of my generation's children were often able to use computers before they could read.

The examples I have given of change involve technology, perhaps the most visible and easily comprehensible dimension of change in our lives. However, these technological changes have also produced major cultural shifts. They have altered how we experience the world, process information, connect with others, and even perceive and define reality. New "gadgets" impact the way we live in the world and deal with the world. They affect our view of life and even the meaning of our lives.

Discernment then is not about figuring out what is fixed. It is not looking for the eternal amid the changes and chances of life. Rather, discernment involves living with and even embracing change. It means learning to dance with the changes. Such dancing is improvisational. There is no fixed choreography, no unchanging steps.

Improvisation requires being attuned to whatever is in one's environment—the music, other dancers, the space available, objects in that space—as well as one's own body and its rhythms and possibilities. So too with discernment: Our ability to discern means that we pay attention to environment, the cultural context in which we live, as well as to ourselves. Such attention does not mean either that we conform ourselves to what the culture puts before us as valuable nor that we embrace our own wants indiscriminately.

Discernment requires that we be both attuned and critical, that we pay attention to what seems to call to us but also evaluate such inclinations by whether they are indeed life-giving for the world. Just as the ability to do improvisation requires training and skill, our ability to discern is rooted in developing our capacities for attention and critical assessment.

Prayer and Action

In this process, we seek life. Our faith is in God as life-giving. The measures of that faith are the authenticity, commitment, and care with which we live our lives. Fullness of life includes prayer and action, not as separate or opposed activities but as modes of being. Prayer and worship flow into action, and action in turn returns us to more reflection and nurturing connection.

If prayer and worship are primary ways through which we engage with the divine, then through them we participate in divine power. Both prayer and action are expressions of power. Prayer and worship are intended to give us power for life, individually and collectively. This is most concretely manifest in the ritual of communion: Worshipers partake of the bread of life. They are literally fed and nurtured in the communion service. The Eucharist is meant to provide sustenance for their lives. A concluding prayer in the Episcopal Church liturgy states: "send us out to do the work you have given us to do."

Prayer and worship thus move into action, to work in the world. The people who are empowered by worship in turn empower others. They do the work of God, which includes creating, supporting, and sustaining life in the world. Their action is work for justice, peace, and fullness of life in the world. Action is both expression of power and an act of empowerment.

There is no one way to pray, worship, or act. There is no one right way to be in the world, nor one right way to be in relation to God. There are, however, modes of prayer and action that are disempowering and do not contribute to right relation and life in and for the world.

The Power of God and Our Power

The question—whose side is God on?—is probably one that most people have asked, in one form or another, at some point in their lives. As I have tried to make clear, the answer is: God is on the side of life.

This affirmation does not mean that bad things do not happen. Nor does it mean that violence and harm are not part of life. It does mean, however, that the divine seeks life.

God is power for life. Such power does not dominate or control. It does not even manage or direct. We need not submit to it. Our prayer then is not to be conformed to God's will but to be open and receptive to life-giving power. When we pray we are seeking empowerment.

The God to whom we pray, the image we hold of God, the metaphors that speak to us, may be, and ought to be, multiple. There is no one metaphor that is true in any absolute sense. I would venture to say there is no one metaphor that we can count on to be right in all circumstances. No one size fits all.

The measure of truth or rightness is not the metaphor itself but whether our connection, our prayer, and our action, are life-giving. There may be times when finding comfort in a nurturing image of God feeds us. Other times when understanding God as the energy that makes and keeps life going fuels our own action in the world. Yet other times it may help to know that God suffers with us or that God is mighty in the face of what seems like prevailing evil.

At the same time we might take care not to foster metaphors for God that seem to curtail life, that put a chokehold on people's ability to claim fullness of life. Metaphors that stress God's power as controlling and dominating are particularly prone to such distortions of life-giving power.

In this process of discernment, we must also be careful that we do not simply make God whatever we want God to be—the answer to our prayers, so to speak, meeting our needs and fulfilling our desires. In this complex, interwoven universe of ours, it is so easy for self-centeredness to curtail the possibilities of life for others. Prayer is first and last about life for the world, life for the whole universe.

This is the adventure of faith: becoming ourselves more and more aware of the whole that is endless and ever beyond our knowing fully. The word *adventure* includes "advent" which means "coming to." In this life we are ever coming to life and life is ever coming to us. The encounter with God is eternal advent. We pray for openness to that coming, openness to life. May the energy at the heart of all, ever dynamic and connecting, abound. May life renew itself again and again.

> O divine spark, heartbeat of creation,
> Pulsing the cosmos into rhythmic tides
> Of life and love, love and life
> Flourishing
> In and for all, now and forever.

NOTES

Introduction

The article about Kayla's death, "Seekonk shocked at teen's death in riding accident" by Alisha A. Pina, appeared in the *Providence Journal* on February 19, 2005.

Harold S. Kushner's book, *When Bad Things Happen to Good People*, was published by Avon Books in 1983.

2. Lord and Master

Hymns cited: #410, 414 and 450 in *The Hymnal 1982* (New York: Church Hymnal, 1985).

4. The Prodigal Son Revisited

Hymns cited: #439, 304, 377, 671, and 676 in *The Hymnal 1982* (New York: Church Hymnal, 1985).

5. Friendly Persuasion

Hymns cited: #423 and 654 in *The Hymnal 1982* (New York: Church Hymnal, 1985).

6. Your Pain Is My Pain

For Moltmann's ideas about suffering and God, see Jürgen Moltmann, *The Crucified God*, trans. R. A. Wilson and John Bowden (New York: Harper & Row, 1974).

The citation from Elie Wiesel's *Night*, trans. Stella Rodway (New York: Bantam, 1982), is on page 62.

Hymn cited: #448 in *The Hymnal 1982* (New York: Church Hymnal, 1985).

7. Power with Us

Dietrich Bonhoeffer's reflections about God, human beings, and the changing nature of Christianity are sprinkled throughout his *Letters and Papers from Prison*, ed. Eberhard Bethge (New York: Macmillan, 1972).

Carter Heyward's ideas about God as the power in relation, erotic power, and "godding" may be found throughout her work. See especially, *Touching Our Strength: The Erotic as Power and the Love of God* (San Francisco: Harper & Row, 1989) and *Our Passion for Justice: Images of Power, Sexuality, and Liberation* (New York: Pilgrim, 1984).

Another feminist theologian who emphasizes relationality and erotic power is Rita Nakashima Brock, *Journeys by Heart: A Christology of Erotic Power* (New York: Crossroad, 1988).

Paul S. Fiddes's theology is presented in *Participating in God: A Pastoral Doctrine of the Trinity* (Louisville: Westminster John Knox, 2000).

Hymn cited: #423 in *The Hymnal 1982* (New York: Church Hymnal, 1985).

8. Power in Us

Paul Tillich's ideas about being may be found in his *Systematic Theology*, Vol. 1 (Chicago: University of Chicago Press, 1951).

Karl Rahner's ideas may be found in *Foundations of Christian Faith*, trans. William V. Dych (New York: Seabury, 1978).

Hymns cited: #501 and 506 in *The Hymnal 1982* (New York: Church Hymnal, 1985).

FOR FURTHER READING

Bloesch, Donald G. *God the Almighty: Power, Wisdom, Holiness, Love*. Christian Foundations Series. Downers Grove, Ill.: InterVarsity, 1995. A discussion of who God is and how God acts, written by a leading evangelical theologian. Bloesch positions himself in relation to other more liberal theologians such as Sallie McFague and Jürgen Moltman, with an emphasis on God's power and sovereignty.

Borg, Marcus J. *The God We Never Knew: Beyond Dogmatic Religion To A More Authenthic Contemporary Faith*. San Francisco: HarperOne, 1998. A popular author, drawing from his own spiritual journey, writes about a panentheistic God who might speak to people who are looking for a more life-giving relationship with God in the context of the world today.

Carroll, B. Jill. *The Savage Side: Reclaiming Violent Models of God*. Lanham, Md.: Rowman & Littlefield, 2001. Carroll looks at the fiction of Annie Dillard to develop a nature theology that argues, against feminist theologians such as Sallie McFague, that God has an indifferent and even savage side.

Christ, Carol P. *She Who Changes: Re-Imagining the Divine in the World*. New York: Palgrave Macmillan, 2003. Christ builds on her earlier work and draws on process thought to present a theology of the Goddess, fully present in the world, relational, connected, and changing.

Cobb, John B. *God and the World*. Philadelphia: Westminster, 1969. An early and introductory work by a leading process theologian discussing God and God's relation to the world.

Erickson, Millard J. *God the Father Almighty: A Contemporary Exploration of the Divine Attributes*. Grand Rapids, Mich.: Baker, 1998. A traditional, conservative evangelical approach to the nature and activities of God intended to refute contemporary challenges.

Fiddes, Paul. *Participating in God: A Pastoral Doctrine of the Trinity*. Louisville, Ky.: WestminsterJohnKnox, 2000. A lively approach to the Trinity as relationship and the implications of that model for other theological topics. Fiddes emphasizes participation to connect ideas about God to the life and practices of Christian community.

Frielingsdorf, Karl. *Seek the Face of God: Discovering the Power of Your Images of God*. The Ignatian Impulse Series. Notre Dame, Ind.: Ave Maria, 2006. In an engaging and accessible style, a Jesuit psychologist surveys a variety of images of God, how they are rooted in people's early experiences, and the difference they make for spirituality and how people live their lives.

Friesen, Garry, with J. Robin Maxson. *Decision Making and the Will of God: A Biblical Alternative to the Traditional View*. Portland, Ore.: Multnomah, 1980. Friesen, taking on the most deterministic views of God's will, presents a view of God's will as directing but that still leaves room for human freedom.

Heyward, Carter. *Our Passion for Justice: Images of Power, Sexuality and Liberation*. New York: Pilgrim, 1984. A collection of essays that contain Heyward's critiques of theologies of domination and offer ideas about God as relational.

Johnson, Elizabeth A. *She Who Is: The Mystery of God in Feminist Theological Discourse*. New York: Crossroad, 1992. A Roman Catholic feminist theologian presents a theology of God in which God is fully relational, enters into suffering, and empowers for liberation.

Kaufman, Gordon. *God the Problem*. Cambridge, Mass.: Harvard University Press, 1972. An examination of contemporary issues and concerns regarding who God is and how God acts, with attempts to construct a more fitting theology of God.

Kitamori, Kazoh. *Theology of the Pain of God*. Richmond, Va.: John Knox Press, 1965. An early and influential book that developed the idea that God experiences the pain of those who suffer and suffers with them.

Lakoff, George and Mark Johnson. *Metaphors We Live By*. 2nd ed. Chicago: University of Chicago Press, 1980. A discussion of metaphor and how metaphors function in society.

McFague, Sallie. *Metaphorical Theology: Models of God in Religious Language.* Minneapolis, Minn.: Fortress Press, 1982. An introduction to theological language as metaphorical and the application of that approach to models of God and Trinity that are more inclusive.

_____. *Models of God: Theology for an Ecological, Nuclear Age.* Minneapolis, Minn.: Fortress Press, 1987. A further development of McFague's metaphorical theology, which draws on contemporary science and its worldviews to do theology specifically in relation to challenges posed by ecological and nuclear threats.

McWilliams, Warren. *The Passion of God: Divine Suffering in Contemporary Protestant Theology.* Macon, Ga.: Mercer University Press, 1985. McWilliams surveys six contemporary theologians, including Kitamori and Moltmann, who propose that God suffers. He also discusses the implications of suffering for the nature of God, including questions of God's power and love.

Miles, Jack. *God: A Biography.* New York: Vintage, 1996. Miles presents the life story of the God of the Hebrew scripture in all its complexity, including God's personality and motivations and the various ways in which God acts.

Moltmann, Jürgen. *The Crucified God: The Cross of Christ as the Foundation and Criticism of Christian Theology.* Trans. R. A. Wilson and John Bowden. New York: Harper & Row, 1974. Moltmann's Christology in which he develops the idea of suffering in God, including the participation of the persons of the Trinity in the event of the cross.

O'Murchu, Diarmund. *Quantum Theology: Spiritual Implications of the New Physics.* New York: Crossroad, 2004. Writing in an accessible style, O'Murchu draws on principles derived from quantum physics and contemporary science to reimagine key theological concepts.

Pinnock, Clark H. *Most Moved Mover: A Theology of God's Openness.* Grand Rapids, Mich.: Baker, 2001. One of the leading evangelical theologians today, Pinnock embraces free will theism and revisits ideas about God's sovereignty and power to present a view of God as fully loving, open to change, and entering into suffering.

Smith, M. Blaine. *Knowing God's Will: Finding Guidance for Personal Decisions.* 2nd edition. Downers Grove, Ill.: InterVarsity, 1991. Presentation, written in an easy style and from a pastoral perspective, of a classic evangelical approach to knowing God's will for individual lives as well as for the world. Since Smith and Friesen (see above) disagree on how God's will operates, this book includes a response to Friesen.

Soelle, Dorothee. *Theology for Skeptics: Reflections on God.* Trans. Joyce L. Irwin. Minneapolis, Minn.: Fortress Press, 1995. A political theologian reflects on different approaches to God and advocates for a God of justice.

_____. *Thinking about God: An Introduction to Theology.* Trans. John Bowden. Valley Forge, Pa.: Trinity International, 1990. In a series of essays, Soelle outlines and demonstrates different approaches, which she labels orthodox, liberal, and radical, to key theological issues and that provide a helpful introduction and comparison.

van Wijk-Bos, Johanna W. H. *Reimagining God: The Case for Scriptural Diversity.* Louisville, Ky.: WestminsterJohnKnox, 1995. A study book that looks at the variety of images for God that can be found in scripture with the intent of moving away from exclusively male images.

Walsch, Neale Donald. *What God Wants: A Compelling Answer to Humanity's Biggest Question.* New York: Atria, 2005. A quick read, by a popular writer, that seeks to reimagine God's will and what it is God wants. Neale answers his own question: God wants nothing.

INDEX

Augustine, Saint, 37, 73, 74

Bonhoeffer, Dietrich, 114, 124, 128–29

Calvin, John, 73, 75
chance, 36–37, 140
compassion, 117–25
cooperation, 101–2
creation, 58–59, 138

dependency, 75–76
discernment, 141, 171–74
dualism (moral), 126, 145–146, 156–157, 158, 167

Einstein, Albert, 14–15, 99, 152
eros, 136, 146. *See also* Heywood, Carter.

Fiddes, Paul, 144
feminist theology/theologians, 13–14, 42, 130, 131, 132–33, 135–36
freedom, 36–37, 98–99

God
    as all powerful, 29–49, 51, 67, 72, 104
    as changeable, 91–94
    as compassionate, 117–25
    as directing and controlling, 59–60

dualistic views, 109–12
as energy, 148–68, 169
    divine, 153, 166, 167
    and power, 158–61
    and reality, 151–53
as good and loving, 38–41
imaging, 11–27
as judging and punishing, 61–63
language for, 26–27
as liberator, 41–43
as light, 164
as magician, 43
as merciful, 63–64, 69–86
as monarch, 30–32, 46–49
mystery of, 17, 145, 166
as nurturing parent, 95–106
as omnipotent, 33
parent metaphors
    biblical sources, 89–91
    nurturing, 87–106
as patriarchal, 51, 56–68, 94
presence of, 132–33
providence of, 60–61, 81
as relationship. *See* God, in relationship.
in relationship, 94–95, 127–46
as teacher, 100–101
transcendent, 16, 154–56
God's will
    as absolute, 59
    as changeable, 92–94
    conforming to, 82–83